DATE DUE

FOLLETT

SHOULD THERE BE LIMITS TO FREE SPEECH?

Laura K. Egendorf, *Book Editor*

Daniel Leone, *President*
Bonnie Szumski, *Publisher*
Scott Barbour, *Managing Editor*
Helen Cothran, *Senior Editor*

San Diego • Detroit • New York • San Francisco • Cleveland
New Haven, Conn. • Waterville, Maine • London • Munich

© 2003 by Greenhaven Press. Greenhaven Press is an imprint of The Gale Group, Inc., a division of Thomson Learning, Inc.

Greenhaven® and Thomson Learning™ are trademarks used herein under license.

For more information, contact
Greenhaven Press
27500 Drake Rd.
Farmington Hills, MI 48331-3535
Or you can visit our Internet site at http://www.gale.com

LIBRARY OF CONGRESS CATALOGING-IN-PUBLICATION DATA

Should there be limits to free speech? / Laura K. Egendorf, book editor.
    p. cm. — (At issue)
Includes bibliographical references and index.
ISBN 0-7377-1429-8 (lib. : alk. paper) — ISBN 0-7377-1430-1 (pbk. : alk. paper)
    1. Freedom of speech—United States—Popular works. I. Egendorf, Laura K., 1973– . II. At issue (San Diego, Calif.)
KF4772.Z9 S54 2003
342.73'0853—dc21   2002034729

Printed in the United States of America

Contents

Introduction

In the 1969 court case *Tinker v. Des Moines Independent Community School District*, the U.S. Supreme Court ruled that students in public schools are entitled to First Amendment rights, provided their methods of free expression are not disruptive or vulgar. According to the majority opinion, written by Justice Abe Fortas, "It can hardly be argued that either students or teachers shed their constitutional rights to freedom of speech or expression at the schoolhouse gate." Nearly two decades later, in the 1988 *Hazelwood School District v. Kuhlmeier* case, the court revised its stance and ruled that public school administrators can censor student speech in newspapers, yearbooks, and other official school publications, even if the speech is not disruptive or indecent. In that decision, Justice Byron White argued: "[We] hold that educators do not offend the First Amendment by exercising editorial control over the style and content of student speech in school-sponsored expressive activities so long as their actions are reasonably related to legitimate pedagogical concerns." These concerns include teachers' abilities to instruct their classes and the orderly operation of schools. As a result of *Hazelwood*, censorship in public schools has become commonplace. In addition, even though college newspapers were not technically affected by the *Hazelwood* decision, they too have been repeatedly censored.

Not all public school students face censorship, however. According to the Student Press Law Center—a legal assistance agency that educates high school and college students about their First Amendment rights—Arizona, California, Colorado, Iowa, Kansas, and Massachusetts have passed anti-*Hazelwood* laws that protect student free expression rights, while Pennsylvania and Washington have regulations that guard against censorship.

Of course, high schools in other states are affected by *Hazelwood*. Two incidents of high school newspaper censorship—though not the only ones that year—occurred in 2002. In February, the principal of an Arizona high school confiscated the current issue of the school newspaper because it included a commentary by an African American student on discord among her fellow African American students. The following month, the principal at a Washington, D.C., high school instructed the student staff to remove stories about the off-campus fatal shootings of two students, because he felt the articles placed the school in a bad light.

Many high school students have sought to avoid censorship by publishing on the Internet. Some students publish independently, while others write for larger web publications. Yet even in these cases, students can still be punished for taking advantage of their free speech rights. In March 1995, high school officials in Bellevue, Washington, decided to withdraw their recommendation that a student be considered for a National Merit scholarship after he posted a parody of the school newspaper on his personal website.

5

Although many educators and their advocates contend that limitations on high school students' free speech is justified in order to protect minors from potentially inappropriate material, First Amendment activists maintain that censorship contradicts an important aim of education—to encourage the exploration of different, even controversial, viewpoints. In an article for the *National Catholic Reporter*, John L. Allen Jr. writes: "Censorship tells kids we want mediocrity, not excellence. The better journalists students become, the more they probe, question and speak out, and the more likely an administrator is to snap them back."

Unlike high school students, nearly all students who work for college newspapers are legal adults; therefore, censorship of college newspapers cannot be justified as a way to protect minors. Nonetheless, newspaper censorship occurs throughout colleges and universities. As in high schools, some of these decisions are made at an administrative level. For example, the administration at Roger Williams University in Rhode Island pulled a spring 2002 column from the student newspaper because it believed the story did not offer a balanced portrayal of the student body.

However, most censorship at the college level occurs at the hands of other students. These acts of censorship typically take less-than-legal forms. Nevertheless, the goal is the same—to prevent stories that might show certain students or groups in a bad light from reaching a wider audience. Newspaper thefts, prompted by the publishing of articles that are found offensive by different segments of the student body, have occurred with alarming frequency since the 1990s. Twenty-five thefts were reported in the 2001–2002 academic year. In one such incident, Temple University freshman Preshal Iyar confessed to stealing (with the help of an accomplice) eighteen thousand copies of the student newspaper after the paper published a story about Iyar's arrest for mail fraud. Iyar was sent to the university disciplinary committee. In April 2002, one thousand copies of the Texas Christian University newspaper were stolen, most likely because of two articles: one on fraternity hazing and the other concerning a player on the women's basketball team who had been accused of using a teammate's credit cards without consent.

At the same time, college newspaper staffs are not always immune from self-censorship. Advertisements that are considered too controversial are often denied publication. One incident that received considerable attention occurred in spring 2001 when conservative columnist David Horowitz submitted an advertisement to forty-eight college newspapers across the country, titled "Ten Reasons Why Reparations for Slavery Are a Bad Idea—And Racist Too." Only fourteen college newspapers published the ad, and several of those who did so later apologized. Among the newspapers that declined to use the ad were the *Harvard Crimson* and the University of Virginia's *Cavalier Daily*. However, conservatives are not the only ones whose right to free speech is ignored; censorship also occurs at right-wing colleges, whose newspapers have rejected advertisements that assert abortion is not murder.

The debate on whether limits on free speech can be justified extends far beyond the high school and college newsroom. As the above examples show, censorship occurs for a number of reasons, from the trivial to the personal to the political. Political speech may get the most attention, but the actions taken at many high schools in the wake of *Hazelwood* show that speech does not have to be overtly inflammatory in order to be restricted. Regardless of the reasons, the infringement of campus free speech—and free speech outside the educational system—continues to be a controversial issue. In *Should There Be Limits to Free Speech? At Issue*, the authors consider whether speech should ever be completely unfettered.

1

Free Speech Is Not an Absolute Right

Cass R. Sunstein

Cass R. Sunstein is a professor at the University of Chicago Law School and the author of seventeen books, including Designing Democracy: What Constitutions Do *and* Democracy and the Problem of Free Speech.

Governments have many legitimate reasons to regulate speech. For example, governments have made perjury illegal in an attempt to guarantee that trials are conducted fairly. The promotion of democratic goals is also a reason why government might choose to regulate television, radio, and the Internet. Requiring television stations to give free time to political candidates, for example, promotes the expression of diverse views. However, political speech is entitled to the highest level of protection because governments cannot be wholly trusted to impartially control speech that may affect their own interests.

There should be no ambiguity on the point: free speech is not an absolute. The government is allowed to regulate speech by imposing neutral rules of property law, telling would-be speakers that they may not have access to certain speech outlets. But this is only the beginning. Government is permitted to regulate unlicensed medical advice, attempted bribery, perjury, criminal conspiracies ("Let's fix prices!"), threats to assassinate the president, criminal solicitation ("Might you help me rob this bank?"), child pornography, false advertising, purely verbal fraud ("This stock is worth a hundred thousand dollars"), and much more. Many of these forms of speech are not especially harmful. A ridiculous and doomed attempt to entice someone to commit a crime, for example, is still criminal solicitation: a pitifully executed attempt at fraud is still fraud. It is possible for reasonable people to disagree with the view, settled as a matter of current American law (and that of most other nations as well), that these forms of speech are all unprotected by the free speech principle. But it is not possible for reasonable people to believe that each of these forms of speech should be protected by that principle. If one or more of these forms of speech is regulable, free speech absolutism is something of a fraud, masking the real issues that must be confronted in separating protected from unprotected speech.

Different types of speech

This is not the place for a full account of the reach of the First Amendment of the Constitution. But it is plain that some distinctions must be made between different kinds of speech. We might, for example, distinguish between speech that can be shown to be quite harmful and speech that seems relatively harmless. As a general rule, the government should not be able to regulate the latter. We might also distinguish between speech that bears on democratic self-government and speech that does not; certainly an especially severe burden should be placed on government efforts to regulate political speech. Less simply, we might want to distinguish among the kinds of lines that government is drawing, in terms of the likelihood that government is acting on the basis of illegitimate reasons.

These ideas could be combined in various ways, and indeed the fabric of modern free speech law in America reflects one such combination. Despite the increasing prominence of the idea that the free speech principle requires unrestricted choices by individual consumers, the Court continues to say that political speech receives the highest protection and that government may regulate (for example) commercial advertising, obscenity, and libel of ordinary people without meeting the especially stringent burden of justification required for political speech. But for present purposes, all that is necessary is to say that no serious scholar really believes that the free speech principle, or the First Amendment, is an absolute. We should be very thankful for that.

No serious scholar really believes that the free speech principle, or the First Amendment, is an absolute.

There are profound differences between those who emphasize consumer sovereignty and those who stress the democratic roots of the free speech principle. For the latter, government efforts to regulate commercial advertising need not be objectionable; certainly, false and misleading commercial advertising is more readily subject to government control than false and misleading political speech. For those who believe that the free speech principle has democratic foundations and is not about consumer sovereignty, government regulation of television, radio, and the Internet need not be objectionable, at least so long as it takes the form of reasonable efforts to promote democratic goals.

Suppose, for example, that government proposes to require television broadcasters (as indeed it now does) to provide three hours per week of educational programming for children. Or suppose that government decides to require television broadcasters to provide a certain amount of free air time for candidates for public office, or a certain amount of time on coverage of elections. For those who believe in consumer sovereignty, these requirements are quite troublesome; indeed, they seem like core violations of the free speech guarantee. For those who associate the free speech principle with democratic goals, however, these requirements are fully consistent with its highest aspirations.

Free speech in American history

There is nothing novel or iconoclastic in the democratic conception of free speech. On the contrary, this conception lay at the heart of the original understanding of freedom of speech in America. In attacking the Alien and Sedition Acts [laws passed in 1798 that made it illegal to print or speak false or malicious statements about the government], for example, James Madison claimed that they were inconsistent with the free speech principle, which he linked explicitly to the American transformation of the concept of political sovereignty. In England, Madison noted, sovereignty was vested in the king. But "in the United States, the case is altogether different. The People, not the Government, possess the absolute sovereignty." It was on this foundation that any "Sedition Act" must be judged illegitimate. "The right of electing the members of the Government constitutes . . . the essence of a free and responsible government," and "the value and efficacy of this right depends on the knowledge of the comparative merits and demerits of the candidates for the public trust." It was for this reason that the power represented by the Sedition Act ought, "more than any other, to produce universal alarm; because it is leveled against that right of freely examining public characters and measures, and of free communication among the people thereon, which has ever been justly deemed the only effectual guardian of every other right."

In this way Madison saw "free communication among the people" not as an exercise in consumer sovereignty, in which speech was treated as a kind of commodity, but instead as a central part of self-government, the "only effectual guardian of every other right." A central part of the American constitutional tradition, then, places a high premium on speech that is critical to democratic processes and is hardly hostile to government efforts to promote such speech. If history is our guide, it follows that government efforts to promote a well-functioning system of free expression, as through extensions of the public forum idea, are entirely acceptable.

American history is not the only basis for seeing the First Amendment in light of the commitment to democratic deliberation. The argument can be justified by basic principle as well. Consider the question of whether the free speech principle should be taken to forbid efforts to make communications markets work better from the democratic point of view. Some standard examples include educational programming for children, free air time for candidates for public office, closed-captioning for the hearing impaired, and requirements that Web sites contain links to sites with different views. Perhaps some of these proposals would do little or no good, or even harm; but from what standpoint should they be judged inconsistent with the free speech guarantee?

If we believed that the Constitution gives all owners of speech outlets an unbridgeable right to decide what appears on "their" outlets, the answer would be clear: government can require none of these things. But why should we believe that? Broadcasters owe their licenses to a government grant, and owners of Web sites enjoy their rights of ownership in large part because of the law that creates and enforces property rights. None of this means that government can regulate television and the Internet as it chooses. But if government is not favoring any point of view, and if it is genuinely improving the operation of democratic processes, it is hard to find a legitimate basis for complaint. Indeed, the Supreme Court has expressly held that the owners of shopping centers—areas where a great deal of speech occurs—may be required to keep their property open for expressive activity. Shopping centers are not Web sites, but if a democratic government is attempting to build on the idea of a public forum, so as to increase the likelihood of exposure to diverse views, is there really a reasonable objection, from the standpoint of free speech itself?

Regulating political speech

In a similar vein, it is reasonable to say that speech that is political in character, in the sense that it relates to democratic self-government, cannot be regulated without a special showing of government justification—and that speech that is not political in that sense can be regulated on the basis of a somewhat weaker government justification. I will not attempt to offer a full defense of this idea here, which, of course, raises some hard line-drawing problems. But in light of the importance of the question to imaginable government regulation of new technologies, there are three points that deserve brief mention.

First, an insistence that government's burden is greatest when it is regulating political speech emerges from a sensible understanding of government's own incentives. It is here that government is most likely to be acting on the basis of illegitimate considerations, such as self-protection or protection of powerful private groups. Government is least trustworthy when it is attempting to control speech that might harm its own interests. When speech is political, its own interests are almost certainly at stake. This is not to deny that government is often untrustworthy when it is regulating commercial speech, art, or other speech that does not relate to democratic self-government. But we have the strongest reasons for distrust when political issues are involved.

Second, an emphasis on democratic deliberation protects speech not only when regulation is most likely to be biased but also when regulation is most likely to be harmful. If government regulates sexually explicit speech on the Internet or requires educational programming for children on television, it remains possible to invoke the normal democratic channels to protest these forms of regulation as ineffectual, intrusive, or worse. But when government forbids criticism of a war effort, the normal channels are foreclosed, in an important sense, by the very regulation at issue. Controls on public debate are distinctly damaging, because they impair the process of deliberation that is a precondition for political legitimacy.

Third, an emphasis on democratic deliberation is likely to fit, far better than any alternative, with our most reasonable views about particular free speech problems. However much people disagree about certain speech problems, they are likely to believe that at a minimum, the free speech principle protects political expression unless government has exceedingly strong grounds for regulation. On the other hand, such forms of speech as perjury, attempted bribery, threats, unlicensed medical advice, and criminal solicitation are not likely to seem to be at the heart of free speech protection.

An understanding of this kind does not answer all constitutional questions. It does not give a clear test for distinguishing between political and nonpolitical speech, a predictably vexing question. (To those who believe that the absence of a clear test is decisive evidence against the distinction itself, the best response is that any alternative test will lead to line-drawing problems of its own.) It does not say whether and when government may regulate art or literature, sexually explicit speech, or libelous speech. In all cases, government is required to have a strong justification for regulating speech, political or not. What I have suggested here, without fully defending the point, is that a conception of the First Amendment that is rooted in democratic deliberation is an exceedingly good place to start.

Free Speech Must Remain Protected

Charles Levendosky

Charles Levendosky is the editorial page editor for the Star-Tribune *in Casper, Wyoming.*

The First Amendment is the foundation of American liberty. The United States cannot consider itself an open and democratic government if its citizens are not free to read or write what they wish, even if that speech is deliberately offensive or criticizes oppressive laws and government policies. However, with rulings in the past two decades narrowing the free speech rights of students, people who value free speech and political dissent must be willing to fight for the First Amendment in the courts.

O ur nation has the noblest and strongest free speech tradition in the world. This tradition has been the very foundation of our liberty. It would be good to remember that fact—as communities around America wrestle with what should or should not be available on the Internet, whether concerts by rock groups should be banned or not, why speech that demeans others should or should not be outlawed.

A strong tradition

The First Amendment is a fabric that weaves through all our liberties. The warp and weft of this fabric protects our right and ability to govern ourselves. And those who would pull out a thread here or cut one out there do not realize they risk unraveling the entire cloth of our freedoms.

Open government and open records are necessary corollaries of a strong First Amendment tradition. The right to know is imbedded in freedom of speech. How does a nation govern itself if its people are deprived of the right to know? What good is the right to criticize the government if such speech can only be delivered in prison while in solitary confinement?

Our First Amendment tradition protects even speech that is deliberately provocative or offensive. For good reason. In the U.S. Supreme Court decision, *Terminiello v. Chicago* (1949), Justice William O. Douglas noted that civil rights leaders often used speech that "induces a condition of unrest, creates dissatisfaction with conditions as they are, or even stirs people to anger."

When Martin Luther King Jr., spoke in Montgomery, Alabama, in support of the boycott against segregated buses that had been begun by Rosa Parks, he said: "There comes a time that people get tired. We are here this evening to say to those who have mistreated us so long that we are tired— tired of being segregated and humiliated; tired of being kicked about by the brutal feet of oppression. . . . One of the great glories of democracy is the right to protest for right . . ." King's speech was protected by the fabric of the First Amendment. And later, the amendment would also protect civil rights sit-ins and other peaceful but provocative marches.

And so, too, union protests are protected by the First Amendment. And the peaceful demonstrations of any down-trodden group are protected by that great liberty. Eventually, the First Amendment overturned loyalty oaths and threats to employment if one belonged to a disfavored group. And it protected the Vietnam veterans who returned home and burned the American flag to protest a dismal, unpopular war. Our nation protects dissent because it understands that from dissident voices may come a public dialogue that changes the minds of our leaders and the path our country takes.

The First Amendment is a fabric that weaves through all our liberties.

Slip a thread from the fabric, and it may no longer be true.

Few professional journalists or newspapers supported Hazelwood East High School student Kathy Kuhlmeier when she challenged the principal's right to censor two articles in the school newspaper she edited. In January 1988, the U.S. Supreme Court issued a broad ruling against Kuhlmeier and her fellow-students and now school administrators have nearly carte blanche authority to censor student speech. The ruling has even impacted community college and university student publications. Many young journalists who seek work at newspapers no longer understand the importance of a free press. They haven't experienced it during their school or college years. How willingly or effectively will they defend their First Amendment rights or ours?

The efforts of the ACLU

This nation's free speech tradition did not arise accidentally. It took civil liberties groups dedicated to protecting the speech and press liberties spelled out in the First Amendment: "Congress shall make no law . . . abridging the freedom of speech, or of the press . . ." As Samuel Walker has demonstrated so clearly in his 1994 book, *Hate Speech: The History of an American Controversy,* the American Civil Liberties Union (ACLU) must be given credit for its key role in preserving the core meaning of freedom of speech. The ACLU was founded in 1920 specifically to defend this right—not only for Communists and Socialists and liberals, but for everyone, including the Ku Klux Klan.

Without the ACLU's perseverance earlier in this century, it is likely we would not have such a magnificent free speech tradition. In his book, Walker concludes that "the protection of offensive speech has been critical to the pursuit of racial equality, along with defense of the rights of other powerless groups—the Jehovah's Witnesses, Vietnam War protesters, and others."

The ACLU was an advocate for unpopular minorities and those without political clout. In recent years, other groups have added their advocacy for freedom of speech, including the American Library Association and People for the American Way and a number of coalitions to ensure that speech on the Internet remains free.

Pull a thread from the fabric, and some other powerless groups will suffer.

Important Supreme Court victories

During the late 1930s and '40s, the Jehovah's Witnesses, a small persecuted religious group, attacked the Roman Catholic Church with a viciousness that brought states to pass laws against their inflammatory propaganda. The ACLU defended the free speech rights of the Witnesses, and eventually all those state "hate speech" laws fell aside.

Constitutional scholar Henry J. Abraham points out that of the 50-plus cases involving religious freedom and free speech issues the Witnesses took to the courts they lost very few. In winning, they won for all of us.

On June 14, 1943, when America was still involved in World War II, the U.S. Supreme Court issued one of the greatest rulings in favor of individual conscience (*West Virginia State Board of Education v. Barnette*). Three years after it had decided that Jehovah's Witnesses could be forced to salute the flag and say the pledge of allegiance, the high court dramatically changed its position. Witnesses believe that the flag is a "graven image" and their religion forbids them to salute it. The *Barnette* ruling upheld their right of conscience and struck down West Virginia's flag salute laws.

In *Barnette*, Justice Robert Jackson wrote for a majority of the court: "The very purpose of a Bill of Rights was to withdraw certain subjects from the vicissitudes of political controversy, to place them beyond the reach of majorities and officials and to establish them as legal principles to be applied by the courts. One's right to life, liberty, and property, to free speech, a free press, freedom of worship and assembly, and other fundamental rights may not be submitted to vote; they depend on the outcome of no elections."

He concludes: "If there is any fixed star in our constitutional constellation, it is that no official, high or petty, can prescribe what shall be orthodox in politics, nationalism, religion, or other matters of opinion or force citizens to confess by word or act their faith therein. If there are any circumstances which permit an exception, they do not now occur to us." To underscore its decision, the high court announced it on Flag Day.

The ruling sweeps further than the flag salute. It resonates deeply with all those who cherish liberty. We have Jehovah's Witnesses to thank for this victory—and many other persecuted or despised minorities who have secured free speech liberties for us by fighting for them. That's the real lesson.

3

The Media Should Use Better Judgment During Wartime

Thomas Sowell

Thomas Sowell is a syndicated columnist.

In the wake of the September 11, 2001, terrorist attack on America, the media should be more cautious about the news and rumors they report. The media frightened their readers by hyping the anthrax attacks, which followed the attacks on September 11. In addition, by treating the ruling Taliban's claims of civilian casualties as fact, the media are undermining America's war efforts in Afghanistan. The media also jeopardize the lives of American soldiers when reporting American military plans. The media must be objective and report only the facts, instead of dangerous speculation.

The media seem to be doing a major part of the terrorists' work for them. What is the point of terrorism, after all? To get the most bang for the buck from the limited resources at the terrorists' disposal. That means scaring as many people as possible from whatever actual damage you can do. The September 11th, 2001, terrorist attacks were the exception, rather than the rule, in creating huge damage.

Usually, it is a question of getting as much mileage as possible from actions that directly harm a relatively few people, but put fear into the hearts of millions and spread confusion that disrupts a whole society.

Publicizing terrorism

The media handling of the 2001 anthrax attacks was all that the terrorists could hope for. The fourth person to die from anthrax produced front-page banner headlines. Tragic as the death of anyone may be, when you are in a war you do not headline the deaths of four people. More people than that can get wiped out with one burst of machine-gun fire. More people than that died in Andrea Yates' bathtub [Yates drowned her five children in June 2001]. It is obvious that the people to whom the anthrax-laden envelopes were sent were chosen because their deaths would be big news. What the terrorists seem not to have realized was that anyone that prominent was likely to have someone else opening his mail.

The ideal, from the terrorists' standpoint, would be to get more publicity and more fear-mongering without having to actually do anything. This too was accomplished for them by big media coverage of potential attacks and highly publicized speculations as to what might happen next.

Government officials have not been wholly blameless in issuing public announcements of "credible threats" of a wholly unspecified nature. What are you supposed to do when you hear such ominous but unknown threats? Stay home from work? And how do you know that the terrorists are more likely to strike where you work than where you live? Such warnings seem less likely to protect the public than to protect government officials from criticisms that they didn't warn us.

Reporting the truth

The media not only help our enemies at home, but overseas as well. Military operations had barely gotten underway in Afghanistan before American reporters were seeking out every case of collateral damage on civilians from our bombing raids—and were reporting the Taliban's [Afghanistan's ruling regime] claims as if they were facts.

Does anyone know of any war where there were not innocent civilians killed? That is one of many things that makes war so hideous. But you don't get out of a war by pretending that you are not in it. The terrorists put us at war on September 11th. We could bury our heads in the sand and do nothing, but that would not stop them—and others—from inflicting more of the same on us. Our only hope of deterring more such attacks is by killing those responsible and letting others know that it is going to cost them dearly if they try anything like it. There seems to be some hand-wringing among some in the media about whether they can be patriotic Americans and at the same time report the news objectively. But the truth is the truth, regardless of whose side you are on. Sometimes it is hard to know the truth, but you don't get around that by reporting every claim by an enemy regime with a long history of lying—and then pretending to believe that it is just as credible as what you have learned from more reliable sources.

Much of the media has a confusion between being objective and creating an arbitrary "balance" between "the two sides."

Objectivity is about facts. Medical science can be objective about the facts about a disease without being neutral as between the bacteria and the patient. Medical researchers' objectivity about the facts is what enables them to discover how to save the patient's life and kill the bacteria.

News-gathering does not have to stop during a war. But news is what has actually happened. Rumors and speculation are not news. Nor are American military plans news. Reporting these plans and jeopardizing Americans' lives is espionage.

4

Free Speech Should Not Be Restricted During Wartime

Robyn E. Blumner

Robyn E. Blumner is a columnist and editorial writer for the St. Petersburg Times *in Florida and a former director of the American Civil Liberties Union of Florida.*

The American government has a long history of suppressing free speech during wartime, including the Alien and Sedition Acts, which were laws passed in 1798 that prohibited writing or publishing anything false or malicious about the government. Although the government has not passed a similar law in the wake of the September 11, 2001, terrrorist attack, newspaper editors have been too quick to support speech suppression and the loss of other civil liberties. The mainstream press should oppose efforts to weaken civil liberties and work with the court system and political activists to ensure that the United States does not retreat to the actions of earlier wars.

A merican soldiers enlisted in the battle against the forces of al-Qaida and Islamic fundamental extremism may believe they are fighting for the good of the USA and its abiding commitment to liberty. Yet the truth is, war has never been particularly good for liberty. In times of crisis, when the country is infused with fear and anxiety, voices calling for restrictions on civil liberties have often prevailed. It is an odd irony that the defining principles undergirding this nation—free speech, privacy, due process, and equal protection—are often seen as unaffordable luxuries, even unpatriotic nuisances during times of war or other national stress. One has to hope that our current conflict will be the exception, and our government won't adopt its routine wartime stance of imposing guilt by association, silencing dissenters, spying on political activists, and running roughshod over due process. But if history is any guide, the Bill of Rights is in for some difficult times.

A dark history

Even our founding fathers were not immune to this unfortunate impulse. The darkest moment of John Adams' presidency was signing the Alien and Sedition Acts of 1798, laws that made it a crime to "write, print, utter, or publish" anything "false, scandalous, and malicious" against the government. Adams felt, in light of the goings on in France during the French Revolution, the outlandish and irresponsible churnings of the Republican press had to be contained for the good of the country (and his own ego).

Of course, the most notorious examples of presidents assaulting liberties during wartime are Abraham Lincoln's decision to suspend the writ of habeas corpus during the Civil War and the utterly tragic decision by President Roosevelt to commit 120,000 Japanese immigrants and Americans of Japanese descent to internment camps throughout the West during World War II.

Those measures may have seemed necessary then, but with hindsight we view them as mistakes, serious mistakes. The retraction of freedom didn't buy us a bit of extra safety.

These oversteps happen when flag-waving jingoism overtakes public sentiment. Soon, any challenge to government action becomes a sign of disloyalty, and that's when tyrants are given quarter. Men like Woodrow Wilson's attorney general, A. Mitchell Palmer, who was allowed to launch his own personal pogrom against immigrants from Eastern Europe active in the labor movement. Palmer jailed and deported thousands of pacifists whose only crime was their peaceful protest of American involvement in the war.

It is an odd irony that the defining principles undergirding this nation . . . are often seen as unaffordable luxuries, even unpatriotic nuisances during times of war.

In 1917 Congress passed the Espionage Act, a law prohibiting the mailing of any publication urging "treason, insurrection, or forcible resistance to any law." It was used as a way to shut down German language newspapers run by German Americans in areas of rural Pennsylvania, Wisconsin, and Minnesota. During that time, 44 papers lost their mailing privileges and 30 more had to agree not to write about the war in order to continue publishing.

In New York at that time, the Postmaster found "unmailable" a left-wing periodical titled *The Masses*, whose contributors included Carl Sandburg, because its anti-war articles and cartoons "tended to produce a violation" of the Espionage Act.

The Supreme Court and free speech

The judiciary, the one branch of government whose purpose it is to stand up for individual rights against majoritarian pressures, has not acquitted itself well during times of war when we have needed its independence most.

During World War I, courts had virtually no sympathy for claims by publishers prosecuted under the Espionage Act that they were victims of First Amendment violations. For example, in a case where the defendant was charged for suggesting that the capitalists and their war will render Liberty Bonds worthless, the judge told the jury that the First Amendment is no defense "where the honor and safety of the Nation is involved."

And we all know the shameful answer the U.S. Supreme Court gave to Japanese American Fred Korematsu, a man born in Oakland, California, who challenged the constitutionality of his internment during World War II: "Tough!"

There are some encouraging signs that today's court wouldn't be so willing to go along with every government claim of national need. In his recent book, *All the Laws But One: Civil Liberties in Wartime*, U.S. Supreme Court Chief Justice William Rehnquist noted: "It is all too easy to slide from a case of genuine military necessity to one where the threat is not critical and the power either dubious or nonexistent." That's an interesting observation coming from a justice who has so often sided with the government at the expense of civil liberties.

Justice Sandra Day O'Connor wasn't as reassuringly cynical when she said in a speech soon after the September 11 attacks, that America's response may mean "more restrictions on our personal freedom than has ever been the case in our country." She did, however, express the need for caution as we "re-examine some of our laws pertaining to criminal surveillance, wiretapping, immigration, and so on."

Newspapers are rolling over

But what might be most distressing for editorialists is the way so many newspaper editorial pages have repeatedly rolled over during wartime, buying wholesale the need for speech suppression or rounding up people based on their ethnicity for the sake of national security.

According to Joseph McKerns, associate professor of journalism at Ohio State University, who has researched the editorial reaction of newspapers to the free speech baffles during World War I, few editorial boards stood up for civil liberties. Instead, they chose to reflect the xenophobic views of their readership.

"When it came to freedom of association and freedom of speech" said McKerns, "the daily press made a convenient separation, seeing the speech of the political activist as different from what it did." Much of what appeared in newspapers at that time, McKerns said, was highly anti-immigrant: "Even in framing the news, immigrants, the labor movement, and foreigners were the ones portrayed as a threat rather than merely exercising free speech."

The Bill of Rights, embodying the concepts of individual rights and limited government, is only worth the paper it's written on unless those charged with keeping the government honest to its limits are willing to stand up and say so at the most provocative times.

National unity does not mean national goose-stepping. The courts, political activists and the mainstream press—the primary countervailing forces to executive and legislative power—have a special responsibility in times of war to raise their level of vigilance and not give in to nationalistic pressures.

That is the only way this nation now, at this time of heightened anxiety, is going to keep from repeating its undistinguished wartime history.

Poll after poll may indicate that Americans are willing to give up some civil liberties in exchange for more security against terrorism. But they don't really mean it. What Americans mean is that it would be O.K. for people who don't look like them—people who wear headscarves or who sport untrimmed facial hair—to lose some liberty.

That way of thinking cannot be acceptable to the courts or to editorial boards. As editorialists these are our front lines in times of war. The question is, how many of us will stand our ground and how many will desert the field?

5

Public Schools and Libraries Should Install Internet Filters

Bruce Watson

Bruce Watson is the president of Enough Is Enough, a nonpartisan group that seeks to make the Internet safer for children and families.

The ease with which pornography can be found on the Internet shows why filtering software should be installed in public libraries and schools. The Children's Internet Protection Act (CIPA), which requires that schools and libraries that use federal funds to pay for Internet access spend part of those funds on Internet filters, is an appropriate vehicle for ensuring that children are not bombarded with obscene images when they use the Internet. Opponents of filtering software spread false information about the effectiveness of such programs, ignoring the fact that almost all Americans believe that pornography should be filtered out of public computers. While parents remain largely responsible for their children's use of the Internet, the CIPA will provide them with valuable support. This viewpoint was written prior to the May 2002 decision by the federal court in Philadelphia, which ruled that the CIPA is unconstitutional.

How would you feel if your 11-year-old son went down to the public library and checked out *Deep Throat*, the hard-core pornographic video? Or your 9-year-old daughter stumbled across *Hustler* magazine during a research project in her classroom at school?

Most parents would experience something between shock and outrage, plus an element of pure surprise. But, of course, these are purely hypothetical examples—schools and libraries don't offer pornographic magazines and videos to kids. In fact, even for adults, it is almost unheard of for public libraries to have materials such as *Hustler* or *Deep Throat* in their print or video collections.

The spread of Internet pornography

So presumably the same standards also would apply on the Internet, right? The answer, unfortunately, is not yet, which is why Congress took a step in this direction in December 2000 by passing the Children's Internet Protection Act (CIPA). The CIPA offers a simple deal: if federal funds are used to provide Internet access in schools and libraries, then part of those funds must be used to filter out the pornography. (More precisely, child pornography, obscenity and material defined legally as "harmful to minors" must be filtered for minors age 16 or younger. For adult access, only the first two categories apply, with disabling available by a supervisor for research or other bona fide purposes.) Although CIPA was tucked into an appropriations bill, there is no question it was a response to widespread concern: A national survey [in fall 2000] by Digital Media Forum found an overwhelming 92 percent support for filtering pornography out of school computers.

The reasons for concern have little to do with coyly posed *Playboy* centerfolds. Even veteran pornographer Larry Flynt has acknowledged that "There's an awful lot of material on the Internet that children should not have access to. There's material that even I, in my wildest imagination, would not consider publishing." And much of it is freely available to anyone who stumbles onto a porn Website.

The harsh reality is that commercial porn sites now display a host of free materials that are harmful to minors.

A study [in summer 2000] for the National Center for Missing and Exploited Children found that one in four online youths ages 10 to 17 had an unwanted encounter with pornography in the previous 12 months. Children today are encountering these hard-core sites through misleading site names (such as *whitehouse.com*, a porn site), through invisible "metatags" misusing popular brand names such as Nintendo or Muppets, through unsolicited e-mail or simply by typing the word "porn" into an unfiltered Internet browser. Curiosity in children and teenagers is natural and healthy, but the distorted lens of hardcore porn offers a poor sexual role model.

The opponents' falsehoods

So why is CIPA vehemently opposed by groups such as the American Civil Liberties Union (ACLU) and their friends at the American Library Association (ALA)? Their public posture is that CIPA might be well-intended, but technical difficulties make all such legislation unworkable. Closer inspection reveals that the real debate is philosophical.

Opponents of filtering say the software has too many anomalies, such as "overblocking" Websites for chicken-breast recipes or the county of Middlesex. Such examples often are based on first-generation word-association software rather than state-of-the-art products. They reflect the astonishingly persistent disinformation campaign waged by filtering opponents. Other examples, rather than confirming a sinister political agenda, have an almost hilariously random quality, such as the famous (and brief) blocking by one product of the Quaker church Website.

The real question is not whether filters are perfect—if you use Windows, you know that perfection is an impossible standard in the world of computers and, thus, irrelevant.

The real question is whether they work within a tolerable level of error. Experience in schools and libraries indicates that the good brands meet this test comfortably. The performance of the better products is one reason why the number of libraries using filters has doubled in the last two years. Approximately 25 percent of libraries now use at least some filtering, according to the National Commission on Library Science.

Besides, how can today's filtering software be described as a one-size-fits-all solution when the industrial-strength products for schools and libraries typically have between 20 and 60 categories of customization available? Do the math—that's a dizzying range of permutations.

The ACLU/ALA strategy is fairly straightforward: By relentlessly publicizing the "anomaly of the week," they distract attention from the inherent absurdity of their own demand—that only a perfect filter is acceptable in the imperfect world of computers. They would have us believe that a single overblocked site is a more significant anomaly than an entire generation of schoolchildren given free and easy access to the crudest of hard-core pornography. It's easy to see why 92 percent of the public disagrees with them.

The ALA's solution is to promote "acceptable-use policies" in each local library. The only problem is they don't work. More than 90 percent of public libraries already have such policies, yet former librarian David Burt's study, *Dangerous Access (2000 Edition)*, found thousands of incidents of library patrons accessing pornography online. The more disturbing incidents included public masturbation, adults enticing children to view porn sites and trading in child pornography. Burt filed requests under the Freedom of Information Act for incident reports concerning Internet pornography but received only a 29 percent response rate after the ALA got involved. So much for open access to information.

The ACLU and ALA argue that CIPA is too vague because just about anything might be considered "harmful to minors" by someone. However, this legally defined term already is used in the print world, and there is scant evidence of "rogue" prosecutions. The courts have made clear that this term cannot be extended to mere nudity or sexual information, regardless of how controversial the political or sexual viewpoints may be. The harsh reality is that commercial porn sites now display a host of free materials that are harmful to minors or even obscene under almost any standard. The Pink Kitty Porn Palace Website isn't showing AIDS-prevention information or video tours of the Louvre.

The need for legislation

A more serious concern, especially for conservatives, is whether it is necessary for the government to step in and require filtering. Part of the answer is that, if schools and libraries provide unfiltered access only, then

public funds are being used to distribute pornography. When government funds are creating the problem, government funds should provide the solution. Requiring the feds to clean up their own mess is hardly a "big-government" proposition.

Children's safety online involves parents and other gatekeepers, the Internet industry and the legal community.

The other reason for a legislated approach is that the group that could help most—the ALA—is instead leading the opposition. Says Judith Krug, director of the ALA's Office of Intellectual Freedom: "Blocking material leads to censorship. That goes for pornography and bestiality, too. If you don't like it, don't look at it." This applies even for children. Their fetchingly titled manual, *The Censor Is Coming—Intellectual Freedom for Children*, notes that, by formal policy, "the ALA opposes all attempts to restrict access to library services, materials and facilities based on the age of library users." The fierce opposition of ALA's Head Office is the principal reason why 75 percent of libraries use no filtering today.

When communities fret that this ivory-tower approach makes local libraries unsafe for children, Krug responds: "If you don't want your children to access that information, you had better be with your children when they use a computer." Former ALA president Ann Symons explains: "We do not help children when we simply wall them off from information and ideas that are controversial and disturbing." The fallacy, of course, is to equate pornography with information and ideas. Hard-core pornography is simply not an intellectual matter; rather, like the Bill Clinton/Monica Lewinsky affair, the guiding impulse for porn comes from another part of the anatomy.

Another ALA mantra is that government can't censor and, because libraries are government-funded, therefore libraries can't censor. This catchy sound bite is meaningless. Government funds also are used for office buildings, theaters and public parks—each with quite different First Amendment protection. The mantra also ignores the critical difference between the government as sovereign (the king can't restrict his subjects' private speech) and the government as patron (the king does not have to support every artistic or literary endeavor).

ALA dogma

The selective way the ALA applies its own dogma is even more intriguing. [In summer 2000] a Toledo, Ohio, couple contributed a critical biography of Planned Parenthood founder Margaret Sanger to their local library because none of the library's 20-odd books on the subject mentioned her controversial views on race or eugenics. The library declined the gift because "the author's political and social agenda . . . is not appropriate." Contacted by WorldNetDaily for comment, the ALA's Krug—oblivious to the irony—blandly explained that librarians can determine "what materials are useful for their community." This is the same official whose response to community concerns about Internet porn is, "If you don't like it, don't look at it."

Under the ALA's definition of intellectual freedom, it apparently is just fine for government employees (librarians) to exclude materials from a public library because of "the author's political and social agenda," but it would be censorship for private citizens to question the wisdom of providing hard-core pornography. Perchance the ALA has a "political and social agenda" of its own?

Inevitably, CIPA will spend the next few years tied up in legal challenges by the ACLU (and possibly the ALA). The ACLU still trumpets its low-grade win in a Virginia District Court against the Loudon County library. The judge compared filtering to ripping pages out of an encyclopedia, forgetting that any encyclopedia is but a single published work, while the Internet is an entire medium, like TV. (Libraries that provide PBS programming feel no obligation to add the Spice Channel.) For various reasons, the independent *TechLaw Journal* concluded, "The library would probably win before the 4th Circuit Court of Appeals, if it were to appeal."

The library's decision not to appeal was colored by the magnitude of the plaintiff's legal fees if it lost. Even at the district-court level, the fees presented by the ACLU and coplaintiffs People for the American Way were a speech-chilling $488,601, compared to the $55,000 paid to the library's attorneys. Fortunately, such intimidation will have less weight against the CIPA, where the defendant will be the Bush Department of Justice.

In conclusion, it is important to remember that parents still have the primary responsibility for guiding their children on the Internet, just as they do on issues like smoking or drinking. The problem is that parents today carry all the responsibility, even though they usually are less computer-literate than their children. Parents need the support of the law, just as they do with smoking and drinking. Children's safety online involves parents and other gatekeepers, the Internet industry and the legal community. It would be irresponsible for any of these groups to claim a free ride by having someone else shoulder the entire burden.

6

Internet Filters Should Not Be Installed in Public Schools and Libraries

Electronic Frontier Foundation

The Electronic Frontier Foundation works to protect privacy and freedom of expression in the arena of computers and the Internet.

Legislation that forces libraries and schools that receive federal funding to install Internet filters is misguided and violates the First Amendment. Filtering software relies on subjective and biased criteria to determine which websites will be accessible and often blocks sites with no offensive material. Most important, such software causes harm to the First Amendment–protected right to read material that is constitutionally protected for all Americans. In addition, such legislation—in particular the Children's Internet Protection Act and the Neighborhood Child Internet Protection Act—is costly, ignores the capabilities and responsibilities of libraries, forces one system of morality onto the entire nation, threatens children's privacy, and makes no distinction between teenagers and younger children. This viewpoint was published prior to the May 2002 decision by the federal court in Philadelphia, stating that CIPA is unconstitutional.

Around the end of October 2000, Senator John McCain, Representative Ernest Istook, various other legislators, and the White House, cut a deal to include a controversial and misguided mandatory library content filtering "rider" on a major Labor, HHS & Education appropriations bill, H.R. 4577 (which was in House/Senate conference committee for months, and passed by Congress earlier in December.)

Legislators McCain and Istook, among several others, have for three years pushed various versions of legislation to grant Federal Communications Commission (FCC) regulatory control over the Internet and to force public and private libraries (and schools) that receive any of several federal funding sources to install Internet content filtering software, or else be denied a variety of vital federal funding (including Elementary and Sec-

Excerpted from Electronic Frontier Foundation's statement on H.R. 4577 Mandatory Censorware Provisions, December 22, 2000.

ondary Education Act Title III ["Focused On Technology"], Library Services and Technology Act, and E-Rate funds). Istook's version in the House and McCain's version in the Senate were attached to H.R. 4577 before the bill passed to the conference committee. Both were removed with all other "riders" (small bills attached to a large one in hopes that they'll pass as part of the major bill). [E-Rate funds are discounts on technology such as Internet access.]

While the concerns raised, across the political spectrum, about this legislation probably had little impact on the rider removal decision, many expected the censorware proposal to die at this point (until 2001, at least). But, the chairman of the conference committee offered the disputing McCain and Istook the opportunity to hammer out a joint version of the filtering language. This was done, and the new result was put back in the bill. After further refinements to satisfy the President and VP, passage into law is virtually guaranteed at this point, since the larger funding measure has passed with this rider.

[The filtering proposal harms] the First Amendment–protected right to read.

At this juncture, the "Child Internet Protection Act" and "Neighborhood Child Internet Protection Act" (two related provisions of the filtering legislation) will have to be challenged in court, on First Amendment and other grounds.

The legislation is broadly opposed by liberal, conservative and nonpartisan organizations, from the American Civil Liberties Union (ACLU) and the American Library Association to the Eagle Forum and the Christian Coalition. Congress's own Child Online Protection Act Commission rejected mandatory filtering in their recommendations to the legislature in November 2000.

Despite some early religious-right support for the notion of censorware, conservative groups now raise virtually identical concerns with this legislation as their liberal counterparts. A right-wing coalition letter to key legislators stated, "[t]here is growing concern within the conservative community regarding the use of filtering systems by schools and libraries that deliberately filter out web sites and information that promote conservative values. There have been many reported incidents of schoolteachers and administrators targeting . . . pro-life organizations with filtering software to prevent students from hearing alternative approaches to those issues." One begins to wonder just who, outside of a handful of legislators (and censorware marketers), believes in censorware any more.

Problems with the proposal

For several years Congress has sought to impose some form of mandatory or "pseudo-voluntary" content filtering on all public libraries and public schools. The idea seems to sound nice to legislators and to a large segment of the general public, because they simply do not understand how the technology works (and, more importantly, how it fails to work.) The principal problems with the proposal are inherent in the software and services themselves. These include:

(a) subjective filtering criteria, in which a software company (i.e. a government contractor, subject to the First Amendment) gets to decide broadly what is and is not available to some or all library patrons via library Internet terminals;

(b) biased (typically politically-motivated) filtering decisions, in which software company employees or their consultants (who are again covered by First Amendment requirements because they are doing a job for the government), choose to block material that is not even covered by any stated filtering criteria of the product/service in question; such biases have blocked everything from EFF's own site to gay-rights news stories to Christian church Web pages;

(c) harm to the First Amendment–protected right to read, in an unprecedented system in which unaccountable software companies deny access to materials that are constitutionally protected (including material that no court has ever deemed indecent, obscene, or harmful to minors, as well as content not restricted by any legal category at all, such as "intolerant" material;

(d) mistaken blocking of innumerable sites as "pornographic", "violent", "intolerant" or otherwise "wrong", when in fact they contain no such content at all;

(e) mistaken blocking of names, non-vulgar words, and other material due to bad keyword matching algorithms;

(f) overly broad blocking in which entire directory structures or entire Web sites with thousands of users/authors are wholly blocked for content only found on one page;

[Censorware] does not get the job done, and the cost to library patrons' freedom to read . . . is far too great to bear.

(g) alteration of content in mid-stream, often in such a way as to either leave no indication that material has been censored, or to make the material nonsensical because material has been removed (e.g., in mid-sentence); this technique also raises issues of author's copyright-derived rights to control the distribution of "derivative works", when their words are "sanitized" by filtering software;

(h) provision of few (in many cases, no) options for selecting blocking criteria other than those pre-configured in the software; imposition of censorware would effectively force everyone to adhere to someone else's morality, in clear violation of the Freedom of Religion clause;

(i) dismal ineffectiveness at actually doing what they are advertised to do (block out sexually explicit and certain other kinds of content); no filtering service or product on the market has anywhere near even a 90% effectiveness rate, resulting in a completely false sense of security, and a "solution" that fixes nothing at all;

(j) blocking of materials that are constitutionally protected even for minors, as well as for adults;

(k) imposition of technological censorship measures that have already been ruled unconstitutional, in the *Mainstream Loudoun v. Loudoun Co.* [Virginia] *Library* case.

Costly, dangerous, and ineffective

Seth Finkelstein, the programmer principally responsible for the investigation of X-Stop filtering software and its flaws, vital to the landmark *Mainstream Loudoun* victory, observes: "The claims made by censorware vendors are technologically absurd and mathematically impossible. If people argue endlessly over what is art, how can a shoddy computer program ever have an answer? Imagine if a bigoted organization could, at the touch of a button, secretly remove from a school or library all books they deemed objectionable. That is the reality of censorware. This is book-burning on the Internet, by unaccountable blacklisters." In short, censorware simply does not perform as advertised, and substitutes simple-minded algorithms and a faceless one-size-fits-all morality for complex, context-dependent and highly personal human judgement. It does not get the job done, and the cost to library patrons' freedom to read (and authors' rights, as well) is far too great to bear for such a broken so-called solution to a problem (minors' access to inappropriate material) that is, at heart, one of parental rule-setting and oversight, not federal government regulation.

There are additional political problems that arise with such a proposal including:

1) It is an unfunded mandate that will ironically cost libraries more to implement than they will receive in federal funding in many cases (especially once all costs are included, such as software/service price, training, staff time dealing with complaints, consultant & system administration costs, and, of course, litigation).

2) It would usurp the responsibilities, and disregards the capabilities, of local libraries/library boards and state bodies to deal with these issues as local citizens demand. It would turn the Supreme Court–approved "community standards" content regulation system on its head, permitting the Federal government generally, and national and international corporations in great detail, to dictate what is and is not okay to read in city and county libraries.

3) It would impose a "one-size-fits-all" system of morality over the entire nation—precisely what the First Amendment exists to prevent—disallowing parental discretion and upsetting years of local efforts to set acceptable use policies and practices for libraries (over 90% of public libraries already have such policies in place).

4) It would turn librarians into snooping content police, and thereby threatens both the integrity of the library profession, and patron privacy.

5) It would hit hardest precisely those libraries that most need the withheld funding. Inner-city, rural and other low-income libraries would incur the most difficulty and expense to comply with the law, for the least returns, making it a lose-lose proposition.

6) It would use the definition of "harmful to minors" found in the Child Online Protection Act (COPA), which is currently under a federal injunction against enforcement on the grounds that it is most likely unconstitutional (pending the court's final decision).

7) It would "hard-code" into the law requirements for specific technologies that are both ineffective and likely to become obsolete within a very short timeframe (many believe they are already)—technologies incapable of anything remotely resembling human judgement. At the same time, it would disallow measures such as locally-determined acceptable use policies, family education, or future technologies, as alternatives.

8) Last, but by no means least, it poses a severe threat to children's privacy. The law would mandate the (ab)use of monitoring software (which will necessarily entail detailed logs) to track minors' Internet participation. While this is in and of itself draconian, the matter is far worse than it seems at first. Courts are already deciding (as in the *James M. Knight v. Kingston NII School Administrative Unit No. 16* case) that students' Internet logs are matters of public record. It is both ironic and alarming that a law with "Children's Protection" in its title would do more to harm minors than protect them.

The issues, thus, go far beyond the more obvious freedom of expression concerns. In a coalition letter to Congress from 17 educational organizations (including National Education Association, National PTA, and national principals' and school boards' associations) noted, "[w]hile nearly every school in the United States already supervises minors' online activity, promoting the use of technological monitoring software raises serious privacy and security concerns that have not been examined by Congress. . . . Federal filtering mandates disregard local policymaking prerogatives. Instead they require local decisionmakers to select among a few marketable national norms developed as business plans by filtering software companies."

The legislation in more detail

Aside from the general concerns raised above about the legislation as a whole, there are many devils in the details. Some of the most troubling provisions of the bill are outlined below. Problems are listed as they first appear. Many recur later in the legislation, much of which is duplicative of previous sections, principally to make legal challenge more difficult. (I.e., if we challenge the library provisions and have them struck down, the school provisions still stand until separately and successfully challenged on their own, unless a broad enough case can be brought against all of the provisions at once.)

> *The issues . . . go far beyond the more obvious freedom of expression concerns.*

In Title I:
• The "DISABLING DURING ADULT USE" section imposes conditions that in effect require librarians to ascertain that an adult patron's use of library computers is for "bona fide research or other lawful purposes" before they are permitted to disable the filtering software. If something like this should be done at all (which is highly questionable), this is the job of a judge, not a librarian, and is a massive attack on patrons' privacy and right

to read. Worse yet, filtering is not required to be disabled by adult request (even after these impossible criteria are met); disabling is only "permitted", non-bindingly. As if this were not bad enough, the language has a loophole that could easily exclude actual librarians from having authority to turn off filters at all, requiring the approval of library administrators.

• The "GENERAL RULE" provision is worded such that NO ONE—not librarians, not even parents directly supervising their own children—may turn off the filters for a minor, no matter what it might be mis-blocking.

• The "GENERAL RULE" section also mandates that the software be able to block obscenity, child pornography and material harmful to minors. This is physically impossible—no software can determine what does or does not fall into these legal categories (only a court can), and cannot block even most let alone all of such material without blocking orders of magnitude more material than necessary (i.e. anything that *might* conceivably fall into such a category, and lots more besides). Censorware drags a very large net behind it.

• The "DEFINITIONS" section treats all persons under 17 years of age as if they were the same as 4-year-old children, making no distinction between maturity levels. The Supreme Court has already expressed grave concern with this legal concept, in reviewing "harmful to minors" laws. This new legislation raises this problem much more clearly than any previous laws.

• The "EFFECTIVE DATE" section gives libraries and schools only 120 days to comply with the impossible, or begin to lose funding unless they qualify for special extensions.

• The "OTHER MATERIALS" section permits (though does not require) libraries to block even more material (i.e., material that is not legally deemed obscene, harmful-to-minors or child-pornographic.) This is a recipe for outrageous amounts of needless litigation, and political attempts by censorious groups to seize control of library boards.

In Title II:

• Provision (iii) of the "INTERNET FILTERING" section appears to apply its requirements to private as well as public schools.

• The "CERTIFICATION WITH RESPECT TO ADULTS" section makes it clear that libraries are required to filter ALL library terminals even for adults (again, with a literally impossible requirement that the filters block certain legal categories that no software can accurately detect or identify). This section and the related one with regard to minors, require under no uncertain terms that libraries have and "enforce" policies to ensure that filters are on, used, and not bypassed. This turns librarians into spying Internet cops, violating both their own professional ethics and patrons' privacy. Resistant libraries will immediately be punished by the "FAILURE TO COMPLY WITH CERTIFICATION" clause: "Any [school or library] that knowingly fails to ensure the use of its computers in accordance with [the censorware mandate] shall reimburse all funds received in violation thereof."

Stringent and hypocritical policies

In Title III:

• This additional section, the rather inexplicably named "Neighborhood Children's Internet Protection Act", requires stringent acceptable use policies (aspects of which are federally pre-ordained) for local school and library computer usage, in addition to, rather than as an alternative to, mandatory censorware.

• The deceptive "LOCAL DETERMINATION OF CONTENT" section has three major problems, the first of which is that the federal government is in fact establishing standards of what must be blocked even though the section title says it isn't. Secondly, this provision is a blanket encouragement of more conservative library and school districts' violation of the First Amendment with impunity by blocking anything they want. Third, even the vague and lax restraints that there would be on federal dictating of content regulations are put on hold until mid-2001.

• The "STUDY" section is ironic and hypocritical in requiring an NTIA study "evaluating whether or not currently available commercial internet [sic] blocking and filtering software adequately addresses the needs of educational institutions . . . and . . . evaluating the development and effectiveness of local Internet use policies that are currently in operation after community input." This should have been done BEFORE, not after, considering mandatory censorware laws! The study would also make "recommendations on how to foster the development of" more censorware—highly questionable as something to be legitimately done at taxpayer expense.

• The "IMPLEMENTING REGULATIONS" section gives the Federal Communications Commission the authority and responsibility of implementing the new law. This is probably the real, hidden purpose of the legislation—to give the FCC authority to regulate the Internet like it regulates (censors and permits oligopolistic control of) broadcasting. There is big and particularly anti-democratic corporate money lurking behind this measure. The one and only good thing anywhere in this legislation is a requirement for expedited court review, similar to the review provision in the Communications Decency Act, which enabled the EFF/(ACLU)/(CIEC) [Citizens Internet Empowerment Coalition] legal effort to overturn the CDA on constitutional grounds rapidly, before much harm was done.

7

Colleges Should Adopt Speech Codes

Richard Delgado and Jean Stefancic

*Richard Delgado is a professor at the University of Colorado Law School
in Boulder. Jean Stefancic is a senior research associate at the University of Colorado Law School. They are the co-authors of several books,
including* Must We Defend Nazis?: Hate Speech, Pornography, and
the New First Amendment, *from which this excerpt was taken.*

Colleges have many valid reasons to institute speech codes (regulations that ban hate speech). Contrary to the arguments of neoconservatives, these codes are not a waste of time and resources, are
not rejected by largely white communities, do not prevent discussions of racism, do not encourage minorities to behave like victims,
are not classist, and do not institutionalize censorship. Rather,
speech codes have been proven effective in several Western democracies and can help increase dialogue about racism and race relations by enabling members of minority groups to speak without
fear of verbal abuse. Most important, campus hate-speech codes
protect minorities, who live at a disadvantage in American society.

In [the movie] *Babette's Feast*, the French housekeeper for two dour
Protestant sisters living in a remote Danish village where life is hard decides to mark her fourteenth year of working in this repressed environment by preparing a huge feast. Using money she has just won from the
French lottery, she imports turtles, quail, and the finest wines and serves
them at a long table to the sisters and their congregation. But she has not
counted on the experience's novelty: until now, the God-fearing folks
gathered at her table have not touched a drop of liquor or eaten anything
other than dried fish and other plain foods in their entire lives. During
the dinner, they refuse to acknowledge the delectable dishes they are eat-
ing, talking exclusively about the weather, the crops, and God's will.

The response of some neoconservatives to the campus hate-speech
controversy reminds us in some ways of Babette's feast. Lacking a ready
category for what is taking place under their noses, neoconservatives fail

to notice what everyone else sees, or maintain that it is really something else. As with the villagers, ideology plays its part as well. When something happens that conservative thought does not predict, it is forthrightly denied, leading to some strange alliances, as when Babette ends up playing to the returned general, the one diner who allowed himself to appreciate and enjoy the meal.

Here, we examine neoconservatives and the politics of denial. We take a look at mindset and the rhetorical structures and strategies we often unconsciously choose to deal with in an uncomfortable reality and a changing legal environment. The rhetorical and logical structure of the hate-speech debate has been undergoing a slow but inexorable shift. As First Amendment formalism, with its various mechanistic doctrines, models, and "tests," has begun giving way to First Amendment legal realism, both the moderate left and the moderate right, who much preferred things the old way, have changed their ground slightly. Realizing, perhaps, that mechanical jurisprudence and case law laid down in an earlier era will not hold the line much longer, they have been urging that even if First Amendment doctrine permits regulating hate speech, wisdom and good policy counsel against it.

Six arguments characterize what we call the "toughlove" or neoconservative position:

- that pressing for hate-speech regulation is a waste of time and resources;
- that white society will never tolerate speech codes, so that the effort to have them enacted is quixotic, symbolic, or disingenuous;
- that racist expression is a useful bellwether that should not be driven underground;
- that encouraging minorities to focus on slights and insults is harmful because it causes them to see themselves as victims;
- that the campaign is classist, since it singles out the transgressions of the blue-collar racist while leaving the more genteel versions of the upper classes untouched; and
- that the cure is worse than the disease, because it institutionalizes censorship, and "two wrongs don't make a right."

What unites these arguments—which we call the "deflection," "quixotic," "bellwether," "victimization," "classist," and "two wrongs" arguments, respectively—are two themes. The first is that struggling against hate speech is a digression ("the real problem is . . ."), and the second is that the effort reinforces the idea of oneself as a victim, rather than an active agent in charge of one's destiny.

We examine the six arguments, then offer an explanation for why neoconservatives take the positions they do on the hate-speech controversy. We believe that the toughlove crowd opposes hate-speech regulations because vituperative speech aimed at minorities forces them to confront the intuition that slurs directed against people of color are simply more serious than ones directed against whites. This intuition, in turn, threatens a prime conservative tenet, the level playing field. We explain why the First Amendment version of that field—namely, the marketplace of ideas—is not level but slanted against people of color, and why talking back to the aggressor is rarely a satisfactory option for hate speech's victims.

Speech codes are not a waste of time

Many neoconservative writers who have taken a position against regulation argue that mobilizing against hate speech is a waste of precious time and resources. Donald Lively, for example, writes that civil rights activists ought to have better things to do, and that concentrating on hate-speech reform is myopic and calculated to benefit only a small number of blacks and other minority persons. Instead of "picking relatively small fights of their own convenience," racial reformers should be examining "the obstacles that truly impede" racial progress, namely bad laws and too little money.

Other toughlove writers echo Lively's conclusions. Dinesh D'Souza writes that campus radicals espouse hate-speech regulation because it is easier than studying hard and getting a first-rate education. Stephen Carter also has little good to say about the hate-speech crusade, describing it as a digression and a distraction. Henry Louis Gates expresses perhaps the sharpest disdain for anti-hate-speech activism, wondering why this ephemeral subject attracts the attention of so many academics and thinkers when so much more serious work remains to be done. In a cover story in *The New Republic* reviewing *Words That Wound*, Gates, chair of the department of African American studies at Harvard, writes that addressing racist speech does lip service to civil rights without dealing with the material reality of economic subordination.

Hate speech, in combination with an entire panoply of media imagery, constructs and reinforces a picture of minorities in the public mind.

But is it so clear that efforts to control hate speech are a waste of time and resources, at least compared to other problems that the campaigners could be addressing? What neoconservative writers ignore is that eliminating hate speech goes hand in hand with reducing what they consider "real racism." Certainly, being the victim of hate speech is a less serious affront than being denied a job, a house, or an education. It is, however, equally true that a society that speaks and thinks of minorities derisively is fostering an environment in which such discrimination will occur frequently. This is so for two reasons. First, hate speech, in combination with an entire panoply of media imagery, constructs and reinforces a picture of minorities in the public mind. This picture or stereotype varies from era to era, but is rarely positive: persons of color are happy and carefree, lascivious, criminal, devious, treacherous, untrustworthy, immoral, of lower intelligence than whites, and so on.

This stereotype guides action, accounting for much misery in the lives of persons of color. Examples include motorists who fail to stop to aid a stranded black driver, police officers who hassle African American youths innocently walking or speaking to each other on the streets, or landlords who act on hunches or unarticulated feelings in renting an apartment to a white over an equally or more qualified black or Mexican. Once the stage is set—once persons of color are rendered one-down in the minds of hundreds of actors—the selection of minorities as victims of what even the toughlove crowd would recognize as real discrimination increases in frequency and severity. It also acquires its capacity to sting. A white motorist who suffers an epithet ("goddam college kid!") may be momentarily stunned. But the epithet does not call upon an entire cultural legacy the way a racial epithet does, nor deny the victim her status and personhood.

A second reason why even neoconservatives ought to pause before throwing their weight against hate-speech regulation has to do with the nature of latter-day racism. Most neoconservatives, like many white people, think that acts of out-and-out discrimination are rare today. The racism that remains is subtle, "institutional," or "latter-day." It lies in the arena of unarticulated feelings, practices, and patterns of behavior (like promotions policy) on the part of institutions as well as individuals. A forthright focus on speech and language may be one of the few means of addressing and curing this kind of racism. Thought and language are inextricably connected. A speaker asked to reconsider his or her use of language may begin to reflect on the way he or she thinks about a subject. Words, external manifestations of thought, supply a window into the unconscious. Our choice of word, metaphor, or image gives signs of the attitudes we have about a person or subject. No readier or more effective tool than a focus on language exists to deal with subtle or latter-day racism. Since neoconservatives are among the prime proponents of the notion that this form of racism is the only (or the main) one that remains, they should think carefully before taking a stand in opposition to measures that might make inroads into it. Of course, speech codes would not reach every form of demeaning speech or depiction. But a tool's unsuitability to redress every aspect of a problem is surely no reason for refusing to employ it where it is effective.

Speech codes can succeed

Neoconservatives also argue against hate-speech regulation on the ground that the effort is doomed or quixotic. White people will never accede to such rules. Proponents of hate-speech regulation surely must know this, they reason, hence their objectives are probably symbolic, tactical, or at any rate something other than what they say. Lively, for example, writes that the U.S. Supreme Court has consistently rejected laws regulating speech, finding them vague and overbroad. He also writes that the anti-hate speech campaign lacks vision and a sense of "marketability"—it simply cannot be sold to the American people. Gates asks how hate-speech activists can possibly believe that campus regulations will prove effective even if enacted. If campuses are the seething arenas of racism that activists believe, how will campus administrators and hearing officials provide nondiscriminatory hearings on charges brought under the codes? Elsewhere he accuses hate-speech activists of pressing their claims for merely "symbolic" reasons, while ignoring that the free-speech side has a legitimate concern over symbolism, too. Carter is less negative about the motivations of hate-speech reformers, but does question whether their campaign is not "unwinnable."

But is the effort to curb hate speech doomed or misguided? It might be seen this way if indeed the gains to be reaped were potentially only slight. But, as we argued earlier, they are not: the stakes are large, indeed our entire panoply of civil rights laws and rules depends for its efficacy on controlling the background of harmful depiction against which the rules and practices operate. In a society where minorities are thought and spoken of respectfully, few acts of out-and-out discrimination would take place. In one that harries and demeans them at every turn, even a determined judiciary will not be able to enforce equality and racial justice.

The possibility that campus guidelines against hate speech and assault would decrease those behaviors ought to be taken seriously.

Moreover, success is more possible than the toughlove crowd would like to acknowledge. A host of Western industrialized democracies have instituted laws against hate speech and hate crime, often in the face of initial resistance. Some, like Canada, Great Britain, and Sweden, have traditions of respect for free speech and inquiry rivaling ours. Determined advocacy might well accomplish the same here. In recent years, many— perhaps several hundred—college campuses have seen fit to institute student conduct codes penalizing face-to-face insults of an ethnic or similar nature, many in order to advance interests that the campus straightforwardly identified as necessary to its function, such as protecting diversity or providing an environment conducive to education. Moreover, powerful actors like government agencies, the writers' lobby, industries, and so on have generally been quite successful at coining free speech "exceptions" to suit their interest—libel, defamation, false advertising, copyright, plagiarism, words of threat, and words of monopoly, just to name a few. Each of these seems natural and justified—because time-honored— and perhaps each is. But the magnitude of the interest underlying these exceptions seems no less than that of a young black undergraduate subject to hateful abuse while walking late at night on campus. New regulation is of course subject to searching scrutiny in our laissez-faire age. But the history of free speech doctrine, especially the landscape of exceptions, shows that need and policy have a way of being translated into law. The same may happen with hate speech.

The bellwether argument

A further argument one hears from the anti-rule camp is that hate speech should not be driven underground, but rather allowed to remain out in the open. The racist whom one does not know is far more dangerous than the one whom one does. Moreover, on a college campus, incidents of overt racism or sexism can serve as useful spurs for discussion and institutional self-examination. Carter, for example, writes that regulating racist speech will leave minorities no better off than they are now, while screening out "hard truths about the way many white people look at . . . us." D'Souza echoes this argument, but with a reverse twist, when he points out that hate-speech crusaders are missing a valuable opportunity. When racist graffiti or hateful fraternity parties proliferate, minorities should reflect on the possibility that this may signal something basically wrong with affirmative action. Instead of tinkering futilely with the outward signs of malaise, we ought to deal directly with the problem itself. An editor of *Southern California Law Review* argues that anti-racism rules are tantamount to "[s]weeping the problem under the rug," whereas "[k]eeping the problem in the public spotlight . . . enables members [of the university community] to attack it when it surfaces."

When the government regulates hate speech, it enhances and adds to the potential social dialogue.

How should we see the bellwether argument? In one respect, the argument does make a valid point. All other things being equal, the racist who is known is less dangerous than the one who is not. What the argument ignores is that there is a third alternative, namely the racist who is cured, or at least deterred by rules, policies, and official statements so as no longer to exhibit the behavior he or she once did. Since most conservatives believe that rules and penalties change conduct (indeed are among the strongest proponents of heavy penalties for crime), the possibility that campus guidelines against hate speech and assault would decrease those behaviors ought to be taken seriously. Of course, the conservative may argue that regulation has costs of its own—something even we would concede—but this is a different argument from the bellwether one.

What of the notion that silencing the racist through legislation might deprive the campus community of the "town hall" opportunity to discuss and analyze issues of race when incidents of racism occur? But campuses could hold those meetings and discussions anyway. The rules are not likely to suppress hate speech entirely; even with them in force, there will continue to be some number of incidents of racist speech and behavior. The difference is that now there will be the possibility of campus disciplinary hearings, which are even more likely to spark the "town hall" discussions the argument assumes are desirable. The bellwether argument ignores that rules will have at least some edifying effect and that there are other ways of having campuswide discussions short of allowing racial confrontation to flourish uncontrolled.

Codes will not victimize minorities

A fourth argument many neoconservative critics of hate-speech regulations make is that prohibitions against verbal abuse are unwise because they encourage minorities to see themselves as victims. Instead of rushing to the authorities every time they hear something that wounds their feelings, persons from minority groups ought to learn to speak back or ignore the offending behavior. A system of rules and complaints reinforces in their minds that they are weak and in need of protection, that their lot in life is to be victimized rather than to make use of those opportunities that are available to them. Carter, for example, writes that anti-hate-speech rules cater to "those whose backgrounds of oppression make them especially sensitive to the threatening nuances that lurk behind racist sentiment." Lively warns that the rules reinforce a system of "supplication and self-abasement," D'Souza that they distort and prevent interracial friendships and encourage a "crybaby" attitude; Gates that they reinforce a "therapeutic" mentality and an unhealthy preoccupation with feelings.

Would putting into place hate-speech rules induce passivity and a victim mentality among minority populations? Certainly not, for other alternatives will remain available as before. No African American or lesbian student is required to make a complaint when targeted by vicious verbal abuse. He or she can talk back or ignore it if he or she sees fit. Hate-speech rules simply provide an additional avenue of recourse to those who wish to take advantage of them. Indeed, one could argue that filing a complaint constitutes one way of taking charge of one's destiny: one is active, instead of passively "lumping it" when verbal abuse strikes. It is worth noting that we do not make the "victimization" charge in connection with other offenses that we suffer, such as having a car stolen or a house burglarized, nor do we encourage those victimized in this fashion to "rise above it" or talk back to their victimizers. If we see recourse differently in the two sets of situations it may be because we secretly believe that a black who is called "nigger" by a group of whites is in reality not a victim. If so, it would make sense to encourage him not to dwell on or sulk over the event. But this is different from saying that filing a complaint deepens victimization; moreover, many studies have shown it simply is untrue. Racist speech is the harm. Filing a complaint is not. No empirical evidence suggests that filing a civil rights complaint causes otherwise innocuous behavior to acquire the capacity to harm the complainant.

Classist elements of speech codes

A further argument some neoconservatives make is that the effort to limit hate speech through enactment of campus rules is classist. The rules will end up punishing only what naive or blue-collar students do and say. The more refined, indirect, but more devastating expressions of contempt of the more highly educated classes will pass unpunished. Henry Louis Gates offers the following comparison:

> (A) LeVon, if you find yourself struggling in your classes here, you should realize it isn't your fault. It's simply that you're the beneficiary of a disruptive policy of affirmative action that places underqualified, underprepared and often undertalented black students in demanding educational environments like this one. The policy's egalitarian aims may be well-intentioned, but given the fact that aptitude tests place African Americans almost a full standard deviation below the mean, even controlling for socioeconomic disparities, they are also profoundly misguided. The truth is, you probably don't belong here, and your college experience will be a long downhill slide.
>
> (B) Out of my face, jungle bunny.

Lively and D'Souza make versions of the same argument, Lively urging that the codes reach only blue-collar racism and are backed only by academic elites; D'Souza that the rules aim to enforce a "social etiquette among students, while ignoring the higher-echelon racism of meaningful glances and rolling of eyes of university higherups."

Hateful slurs and invectives are a virulent form of inequality reinforcement.

In one respect, the classist argument is plainly off target. Both blue-collar and upper-class people will be prohibited from uttering certain types of slurs and epithets. Many hate-speech codes penalize serious face-to-face insults based on race, ethnicity, and a few other factors. Such rules would penalize the same harmful speech—for example, "Nigger, go back to Africa; you don't belong at this university"—whether spoken by the millionaire's son or the coal miner's daughter. If, in fact, the prep school product is less likely to utter words of this kind, or to utter only intellectualized versions like the one in Gates's example, this may be because he is less racist in a raw sense. If, as many social scientists believe, prejudice tends to be inversely correlated with educational level and social position, the wealthy and well educated may well violate hate-speech rules less often than others. And, to return to Gates's example, there is a difference between his two illustrations, although not in the direction he seems to suggest. "Out of my face, jungle bunny" is a more serious example of hate speech because it is not open to argument or a more-speech response, and has overtones of a direct physical threat. The other version, while deplorable, is unlikely to be coupled with a physical threat, and is answerable by more speech.

Enhancing dialogue

The "two wrongs" argument, which holds that hate speech may be wrong but prohibition is not the way to deal with it, is one of the relatively few arguments that both the moderate right and the moderate left put forward, although they do so in slightly different forms and for different reasons. The moderate left opposes hate-speech restrictions in part because although it detests racism it loves free speech even more. Neoconservatives oppose regulation because it is government (in most cases) that would be doing the regulating, and especially because in the area of speech, governing to them is synonymous with censorship. Gates, for example, writes that "there is also a practical reason to worry about the impoverishment of the national discourse on free speech. If we keep losing the arguments, then we may slowly lose the liberties that they were meant to defend." He also warns that two wrongs don't make a right and laments that our society and legal system have fallen away from Harry Kalven's ideal of civil rights and civil liberties as perfectly compatible goods for all. Lively writes that history teaches that campaigns to limit speech always end up backfiring against minorities because free speech is a vital civic good and even more essential for them than others. Virtually all the authors of the moderate right persuasion (and some of the moderate left as well) cite the fear of censorship or governmental aggrandizement. If we allow an arm of the state to decide what is harmful speech, soon little of it will survive.

One aspect of the two wrongs argument is worth mentioning. The term "censorship" is appropriately attached to regulation by which the heavy hand of government falls on weaker, unpopular private speakers, or else on political dissidents who are attempting to criticize or change government itself. But with hate-speech regulation, few of the concerns that underlie our aversion to censorship are present. Hate-speakers are not criticizing government, but someone weaker than themselves. In prohibiting it, universities are not attempting to insulate themselves from criticism; the political-process concerns over governmental self-perpetuation are not present. The speech being punished is far from the core of political expression—it carries few ideas at all except "I hate and reject your personhood." Indeed, hate speech silences the victim and drives him away. Thus, when the government regulates hate speech, it enhances and adds to the potential social dialogue, rather than subtracts from it.

The effects of hate speech

Why does the toughlove crowd embrace the six arguments that we examined in the last section and found wanting? We believe the reason has to do with the way hate speech casts doubt on a principal tenet of the conservative faith: the level playing field. In First Amendment theory, the name of that playing field is the marketplace of ideas, in which messages and communications of all sorts supposedly vie on equal terms to establish themselves, and out of which, in theory, truth—the best idea of all— will emerge.

The core difficulty that hate speech poses for the conservative mind is, simply, that there is no correlate—no analog—for hate speech directed toward whites, no countering message which cancels out the harm of "Nigger, you don't belong on this campus—go back to Africa." Vituperation aimed at blacks wounds; there is nothing comparably damaging that whites have to undergo. The word "honky" is more a badge of respect than a put-down. "Cracker," although disrespectful, still implies power, as does "redneck." The fact is that terms like "nigger," "spic," "faggot," and "kike" evoke and reinforce entire cultural histories of oppression and subordination. They remind the target that his or her group has always been and remains unequal in status to the majority group. Even the most highly educated, professional-class African American or Latino knows that he or she is vulnerable to the slur, the muttered expression, the fishy glance on boarding the bus, knows that his degree, his accomplishments, his well-tailored suit are no armor against mistreatment at the hands of the least-educated white.

But not only is there no correlate, no hate speech aimed at whites, there is no means by which persons of color and others can respond effectively to this form of speech within the current system. Our culture has developed a host of narratives, mottoes, and presuppositions that render it difficult for the minority victim to talk back in individual cases, and to mobilize effectively against hate speech in general. These include: feelings are relatively unimportant, words hurt only if you let them; rise above it; don't be so sensitive; don't be so humorless; talk back—show some backbone. Stated or unstated narratives like these form part of the linguistic and narrative field on which minority victims must play in responding to taunts and epithets, and of course limit the efficacy of any such response.

And when campus minorities do mobilize for measures that would curb hate speech in general, they encounter additional obstacles. Although our system of free speech has carved out or tolerated dozens of "exceptions" and special doctrines, opponents conveniently forget this, treating the demand for even narrowly tailored anti-hate-speech rules as a shocking request calculated to endanger the entire edifice of First Amendment protection.

Hate speech, then, is individually wounding in a way that finds no analog with respect to whites; there is no effective way for a victim to speak back or counter it, even when it is physically safe to do so; and the most frequently targeted groups evoke little sympathy from society or the legal system when they ask for protection. In other settings, the combination of the three features just enumerated would cause us to conclude that the playing field is not level, but sharply slanted. Imagine, for example, an athletic competition in which one side is denied a powerful weapon (say, the forward pass); in which the other side is permitted to deploy this weapon freely, because the rules prevent the first from doing anything to counter it when it is used (such as knocking down the ball); and changes in the rules are not permitted because this is said to violate the charter that established the game in the first place.

Surely, we would say that such a competition is unfair. Yet, something like that characterizes the predicament of minority victims of hate speech. Conservatives cannot allow themselves to see this, however, since it goes against some of their most basic assumptions, including free competition and merit. We believe this accounts for the contortions and maneuverings among neoconservatives, including some of color who ought to know better. But the problem of hate speech will not go away by merely insisting on ideologically based truths that "must be so," nor by responses that ought to work, much less by blaming the victim or telling him that the problem is all in his head. Hate speech renders campuses uncomfortable and threatening to substantial numbers of students at vulnerable points in their lives. It helps construct and maintain a social reality in which some are constantly one-down in encounters that everyone agrees matter. And it tolerates and creates culture at odds with our deepest national values and commitments.

Coming to grips with hate speech does pose serious problems for a society committed both to equality and to individual freedom and autonomy. But resorting to facile arguments like those discussed in this chapter does little to advance the discussion. Neoconservatives should allow themselves to see what everyone else sees—that hateful slurs and invectives are a virulent form of inequality reinforcement—and join the serious search now beginning for cures to this national disease.

8

Colleges Should Not Adopt Speech Codes

Robert M. O'Neil

Robert M. O'Neil is a professor of law at the University of Virginia in Charlottesville, the director of the Thomas Jefferson Center for the Protection of Free Expression, and the author of the book Free Speech in the College Community, *from which this excerpt was taken.*

Many colleges have sought to regulate hate speech by adopting speech codes. However, these codes have several serious drawbacks. Speech codes are often imprecise, making it difficult to determine code violations. These regulations are also counterproductive because they can create a backlash against progressive opinions, punish the intended beneficiaries of the laws, and glorify racist speakers. In addition, the constitutionality of speech codes is unclear, although several court cases have ruled that these codes violate the First Amendment. However, the most powerful objection to speech codes is that universities are supposed to encourage free inquiry and not limit an exchange of ideas.

The drafting of campus speech codes [has] brought forth the best and the worst from the U.S. academic community. Some of the early policies were quite simply overzealous. Witness, for example, the infamous University of Connecticut rule (struck down by a federal court) which listed as examples of forbidden harassment

> use of derogatory names, inappropriately directed laughter, inconsiderate jokes, anonymous notes or phone calls, and conspicuous exclusion from conversations and/or classroom discussions . . .

If few speech codes were quite so bold as Connecticut's in seeking to reach otherwise protected speech, many were simply vague and open-ended in ways that invited creativity on the part of deans and disciplinary committees. Take the University of Pennsylvania as a case in point. Many Americans wondered in the late spring of 1993 how a Penn undergraduate could have been charged under the speech code for having shouted "water buffalo" toward a group of African American young women outside his dorm window. The code may not hold the complete answer, but it does help. Penn's policy (later narrowed) had been one of the broadest. It simply forbade "any behavior . . . that stigmatizes or victimizes." The premise of the charge seems to have been that calling anyone a "water buffalo," while invoking the proximity of the Philadelphia Zoo, might well "stigmatize or victimize," if that is all one need prove. In the end, the charge was dropped, though only after national ridicule nearly derailed the nomination of Penn's president, Sheldon Hackney, to head the National Endowment for the Humanities.

Difficult definitions

Penn is hardly alone in falling short of precision. Nearby Haverford College adopted a rule that broadly proscribed many types of discrimination, then added with remarkable candor, "precise criteria for identifying discrimination or harassment are hard to establish." Iowa State University defines harassment or hazing as "any act which intimidates, annoys, alarms, embarrasses, ridicules, or produces psychological or physical discomfort." Harvard's policy makes the definition of forbidden harassment largely subjective, since "the experience of racial harassment may not be so clear-cut and can thus be confusing and disorienting." The task of definition is inherently and inescapably difficult.

Even the best of legal minds have been humbled by a drafting assignment which, in fact, many universities did entrust to their ablest scholars of constitutional law. Moreover, some institutions seem to have abandoned the quest for certainty in part because key terms such as *harassment* lacked sufficient consensus or common understanding. Other institutions, feeling an urgent need to act, did the best they could with this daunting task. The issue before us now is whether that best was good enough, either in law or in policy.

A starting point may be to assess the effect of such policies. Opinions differ on the degree to which codes actually succeed in reducing racist and ethnically demeaning expression. Intensive study at the University of Wisconsin–Madison, for example, found modest correlation between enactment of the code and a period of diminished hostile behavior and expression—though leaving open the question of causality. There seems to be no reliable evidence of the extent to which an improved campus climate can be traced or credited to the enactment of a speech code.

There is, moreover, some tentative evidence of two negative phenomena. One is the rise in expectations that may occur among protected groups after adoption of a speech code but that may be largely unrequited if enhanced civility does not soon follow. Thus, even if racial conditions do not deteriorate, there may be a sense of lost momentum among vulnerable groups in the absence of marked improvement.

Even more serious, there is substantial risk of backlash among those at whom speech codes are directed. Such policies may not only fail to change attitudes for the better; they may actually stiffen the resistance of hard-core racists, sexists, and anti-Semites. Dr. Thomas Jennings, in an exhaustive study of three institutions, found some such evidence at Stanford. He reports:

Some students perceived a backlash against "progressive" opinions among a large segment of the University community, and they linked the political correctness debate with the adoption of [the Stanford speech code]. In other words, some "progressive" black students believed that following the adoption of [the code], "conservative" students at the University were empowered to speak out more during a time when it became fashionable (nationally and locally) to criticize political correctness. Some black students believed that racial relations had not changed as a result of [the code], and that relations might have grown more tense and more separate. A black administrator believed that the adoption of [the code] helped galvanize the more conservative political members of campus to speak out about their concerns.

The downsides of speech codes

Speech codes could become counterproductive in two other ironic ways. American Civil Liberties Union (ACLU) president Nadine Strossen has warned that laws against racist speech can create a discretion in their use that makes the intended beneficiaries of such laws "likely targets of punishment"—a phenomenon that actually occurred under the British Race Relations Act during the 1960s. The other downside risk is one of which Strossen also warns—that "censorship measures often have the effect of glorifying racist speakers" to the extent that "racist speakers may appear as martyrs or even heroes." Thus, there is a genuine danger that speech codes may not simply fall short of a laudable goal but in fact may even undermine that goal.

Backlash or not, risks on both sides inhere in taking a highly visible course of action, especially in response to expressed needs and feelings of vulnerable campus groups. The dilemma is acute: If the university adopts a speech code but conditions do not improve (or actually deteriorate), the institution may experience rising and frustrated expectations. If, on the other hand, the university declines to act and race relations deteriorate, it will also be faulted for failing to take the one step that many may believe would have helped.

Under either scenario, little would be gained by arguing (whatever the record would show) that taking the other course would have been no better and might even have been worse. Perhaps all that can be said is that one ought not to embrace a speech code with any certainty of perceptible impact or tangible results. And proponents may well concede that results are not the central goal in any event.

Apart from results, there are other risks of interpretation. Consider a few of the improbable, almost certainly unintended, situations to which some codes have been applied. Among the first cases filed at the Madison campus under the University of Wisconsin's code (all eventually dismissed) were the complaint of a white student that he had been called a "redneck" by another white during a student senate debate and complaints against a campus newspaper for running a cartoon that allegedly offended Christians.

Perhaps the most poignant example of misdirection involved a white dental student at the University of Michigan. He attended the orientation session of a preclinical class that was widely viewed as one of the hardest courses in the second-year program. After the class broke into small groups, he said that "he'd heard that minorities had a difficult time in the course and that he had heard they were not treated fairly." The professor in charge, a minority person, filed a complaint against the student under the speech code. She claimed the comment was unfair and might jeopardize her chances for tenure. The student was unavailing in his plea that he was sympathetic and was only trying to be helpful. After being "counseled" about the existence of the code, he agreed to write a letter apologizing for making such a statement without adequately verifying the allegation (which he said he had heard from his roommate, a black former dental student).

Such experiences do incalculable harm and go far to dispel two claims that code proponents make—first, that such rules are really aimed at the dormitory and the lockerroom and thus need not affect the learning process; and second, that the speech likeliest to be curbed is largely devoid of content or idea. Several of the Michigan cases show how easily rules designed to deal with extracurricular speech may spill over into the classroom. Quite apart from the fact that no campus code seems to have been so limited in its scope, the process of application is almost certain to follow provocative language wherever that language occurs—with classrooms, libraries, and laboratories inevitable sites of controversy.

The proponents' other premise—that hate speech involves no idea or viewpoint—seems even more tenuous. Ideas or beliefs are in fact central to the use of most slurs, epithets, and the like. If there were no message, there would be no threat; we would simply laugh and walk on. The very source of our concern—the reason victims of such language are so deeply hurt and offended—is that ideas of the most pernicious sort are involved, and are intended to be conveyed. Like many challenging and provocative ideas, they are potentially dangerous. Thus it will simply not do to dismiss speech codes as though they were unconcerned with thoughts or ideas or values. There is a fundamental difference between hateful thought and mindless hate. Speech codes cannot address one without reaching the other.

Two basic concerns

One might now observe that such matters as language, scope, effectiveness, etc., are relatively trivial and miss the main issues. Fair enough. Two basic concerns about what's wrong with speech codes remain to be addressed—the one, that they may abridge free speech and thus violate the Constitution; the other, that lawful or not, they are simply measures inappropriate for a university. The two issues are of course interrelated. Each deserves distinct treatment.

The constitutionality of speech codes remains a matter of debate, though such policies have fared poorly in the courts. The starting point is that all public colleges and universities are bound by the First Amendment. That means they must tolerate much speaking and writing that may not be pleasing to many of their students, faculty, alumni, trustees, and others.

Case after case has reaffirmed this principle with regard to student protest, campus newspapers, radical student groups, and outspoken faculty. While private campuses are not directly governed by the Bill of Rights, many pride themselves on observing standards of expression at least as high as those their public counterparts must meet. Thus the guiding principle for virtually all institutions of higher learning is that free speech must be protected, even when the speech for which freedom is sought may be offensive or disruptive or at variance with the campus mission.

Speech code proponents do not simply repudiate the First Amendment or claim a blanket exemption from the Bill of Rights. There are . . . some solid and seemingly supportive precedents. Not only had the Supreme Court in 1942 upheld a fighting words conviction. A decade later the justices sustained state "group libel" laws aimed at racist propaganda and at the groups that disseminated it. (These laws, in fact, had been passed right after World War II largely at the urging of a young law professor, later the eminent sociologist David Riesman. His goal was to arm governments in this country to resist any repetition of the Nazi propaganda that had paralyzed European governments a decade before.)

By the 1980s, there were major signs of change in the courts. Racists in white sheets had successfully challenged many local bans against the Ku Klux Klan and other hate groups. When the American Nazi Party sought to march through the heavily Jewish Chicago suburb of Skokie and city officials denied them a permit, the Nazis (aided by the ACLU) found relief in both state and federal courts. Then at the end of the decade, the Supreme Court twice struck down flag-burning laws because they made criminal the expression of unpopular ideas. So when the testing of campus speech codes began, resort to the old cases was already tenuous. Immediate court challenges were almost certain, given the intense controversy that preceded board action at the major institutions. Those challenges did in fact occur and by the early 1990s had cast substantial clouds over all such codes, at least on public campuses.

Several important cases

There have been at least five cases. One, brought against the University of Connecticut to challenge the "inappropriate laughter" policy, brought an unreported judgment against the code. The three reported federal cases all arose in the Midwest, against the University of Michigan, the University of Wisconsin, and Central Michigan University. They can be treated as a group on the basis of shared constitutional issues. In the fall of 1989, a federal judge in Detroit held simply that the Michigan regents had abridged freedom of speech. The judge looked well beyond the terms of the code in concluding that the policy reached constitutionally protected speech. Especially revealing was the code's accompanying guide, which told students "you are a harasser when . . . you laugh at a joke about someone in your class who stutters" or when "you comment in a derogatory way about a particular person or group's physical appearance . . . or their cultural origins. . . ." This document persuaded the court that "the drafters of the policy intended that speech need only be offensive to be sanctionable." (The judge was assured the guide had been withdrawn before the case came to trial, though no public announcement had ever been made to that effect.)

The key to this judgment was evidence that the Michigan policy had been applied to speech which clearly would have been protected off campus. Notable (along with the case of the sympathetic white dental student described earlier) was the experience of a social work graduate student who expressed in class his belief that homosexuality was a disease for which a counseling program should be fashioned. The student was charged under the code with harassment on ground of sex and sexual orientation. A formal hearing was held. The hearing panel found the student guilty of sexual harassment but not of harassment on the basis of sexual orientation. Despite the partial acquittal, the judge had heard enough:

> The fact remains that the . . . authoritative voice of the University on these matters . . . saw no First Amendment problem in forcing the student to a hearing to answer for allegedly harassing statements made in the course of academic discussion and research.

Several other cases, including that of the white dental student, reinforced the judge's conviction that the policy was overly broad because "the University considered serious comments in the context of classroom discussion to be sanctionable under the policy." The university administration's own consistent reading of the policy thus confirmed its excessive reach.

There is a fundamental dissonance between controlling words and the very nature of a university as a place of free inquiry.

One such judgment would have been nearly fatal to the speech code movement. This court went on, however, to find the policy unacceptably vague; "looking at the plain language of the policy," he concluded, "it was simply impossible to discern any limitation on its scope or any conceptual distinction between protected and unprotected conduct."

Distinct though they are, these two grounds clearly reinforced one another, as is often the case in free-speech litigation. (A simple example may illustrate the difference between vagueness and overbreadth. If a city passes a law that no one may say "hell," "damn," "God," or "Christ" within the city limits, that is quite precise and thus not at all vague. It is, however, clearly overly broad because it bans much speech that is fully protected. If the same city forbade "all speech that is not protected by the First Amendment," by definition the law could not be overly broad. Yet it would be intolerably vague; even experienced constitutional lawyers could not tell with confidence what could and could not be said within the city limits. Thus vagueness and overbreadth are analytically quite different concepts, even though they often accompany and reinforce one another, as in the Michigan speech code case.)

On to Wisconsin. Some months after the Michigan case, another suit was filed in federal court there, alleging that the regents' speech code was similarly unconstitutional. The emphasis in Wisconsin was much more on the "fighting words" rationale for curbing campus speech; the university had insisted the policy was covered by the old Supreme Court case. But the judge disagreed, since "the rule regulates discriminatory speech whether or not it is likely to provoke a [violent] response . . . [and] covers a substantial number of situations where no breach of the peace is likely to result." Thus the fighting words doctrine offered little support to code drafters. Any attempt to validate the code through balancing of interests seemed pointless; to this judge, balancing would be allowed only with respect to laws that were neutral toward the content of speech. That could hardly be said of the Wisconsin (or any other) speech code, the essence of which is to single out for harsher treatment a particular kind of message. Whether the message is hateful does not matter; the point is simply that speech codes limit expression on the basis of the message and are inescapably content-based.

The Wisconsin federal judge addressed another issue that has been persistently troublesome. Proponents of speech codes often claim that racist epithets and slurs claim no First Amendment protection because they convey no ideas. The court responded:

> Most students punished under the rule are likely to have employed comments, epithets or other expressive behavior to inform their listeners of their racist or discriminatory views. In addition, nothing in the . . . rule prevents it from regulating speech which is intended to convince the listener of the speaker's discriminatory position. Accordingly, the rule may cover a substantial number of situations where students are attempting to convince their listeners of their positions.

Finally, there was again the issue of vagueness. The Wisconsin judge reached a conclusion similar to that reached in the Michigan case:

> The UW rule is unduly vague because it is ambiguous as to whether the regulated speech must actually demean the listener and create an intimidating, hostile or demeaning environment for education or whether the speaker must merely intend to demean the listener and create such an environment.

The inherent ambiguity was compounded by the varied approaches that different campuses adopted, and by the contrast between the code's provisions and the examples that accompanied its publication. The judge acknowledged he could have resolved the ambiguity by going one way or the other—but that was a task for regents and lawmakers, not for federal courts.

Two more recent chapters involve quite dissimilar institutions. At Central Michigan University, the men's basketball coach was discharged for using the word *nigger* in lockerroom exhortation of his mostly black team. He went to federal court, challenging both his dismissal and the validity of the university's "discriminatory harassment" policy. The judge found key provisions of the policy unacceptably vague. He had special disdain for the ban on "any behavior . . . [either] verbal or nonverbal behavior . . . intentional or unintentional . . . [that] subject[s] an individual to an intimidating, hostile or offensive . . . environment. . . ." This policy was no clearer than the University of Michigan code which the same court had struck down a couple of years earlier, and fared no better.

The coach's victory turned out to be Pyrrhic. His discharge was eventually upheld on general public employee speech grounds. The court ruled that his use of a racial epithet, even for hortatory purposes, and even acceptably to some of his black players, did not enjoy First Amendment protection apart from the unconstitutional policy the university had invoked. So in the end the coach won the speech code battle but lost the employment war for reasons that always lurk behind such a case.

Of the three reported federal cases, the one from Central Michigan was the only one to reach a higher court. In the summer of 1995, the appeals court upheld the district judge on both counts. The code, said the appeals court, was fatally flawed because it "reaches a substantial amount of constitutionally protected speech. . . . [Its] language . . . is sweeping and seemingly drafted to include as much and as many types of conduct as possible." The university was, however, within its rights to fire a coach for bad judgment rather than bad language. The court concluded:

> The First Amendment protects the right to espouse the view that a "nigger" is someone who is aggressive in nature, tough, loud, abrasive, hard-nosed . . . at home on the court but out of place in a classroom setting. . . . What the First Amendment does not do, however, is require the government as employer or the university as educator to accept this view as a means of motivating players.

Meanwhile, a quite different kind of case was taking shape at Stanford University, site of one of the most widely touted codes. Stanford's code—though never enforced—drew so much criticism during its drafting that the California legislature adopted a law, the so-called Leonard law, holding nonsectarian private colleges and universities to the same student free speech standards as California's public campuses. Since Stanford's code had been the primary impetus for the law, it was hardly surprising that Stanford became its first battleground. A state judge struck down the code, applying First Amendment precepts as the law prescribed. In the spring of 1995, the Stanford administration decided not to appeal, however much it disagreed with the ruling, and the Stanford code passed into history.

The key flaw of speech codes

Meanwhile, the pertinent principles of law off campus were also changing. About the time the Wisconsin case came down, the U.S. Supreme Court took a case testing the constitutionality of a city ordinance that banned, among other symbolic displays, racially motivated cross burnings. To the surprise of many observers, the justices were unanimous in striking down the law, albeit on two quite different theories. Four justices would have set it aside on vagueness principles very much like those we saw in the speech code cases.

The majority, however, broke new ground. For them the key flaw was the law's focus on content or message or viewpoint, even within an area of speech (fighting words) that could have been curbed even without regard to content. The city could have banned the burning of all materials, including crosses, but could not selectively ban only those cross burnings that were prompted by racial bias or animus. That was viewpoint discrimination, which now for the first time ran afoul of the First Amendment even in the context of otherwise unprotected speech.

This decision seemed to sound the death knell for most campus speech codes. The University of Wisconsin regents, who were struggling to repair or revive their code after losing in federal court, abandoned the effort in September. On a close vote, with vigorous dissent, the regents accepted the advice of their attorney that even a revised code might well abridge free speech. Other institutions also read a clear message, that few codes drawn along such lines could survive the Supreme Court's broader First Amendment ruling. Many colleges and universities either repealed speech codes or allowed them to languish.

A few universities, still committed to such efforts, sought to adapt to the changing law. Michigan continued for some time trying to revise its code, though placing greater emphasis on conduct and not speech. Rutgers, which had adopted one of the strongest codes, now limited the reach of the policy to speech that could be criminally punished under state law. But most of the codes were either given a decent burial by formal action or were allowed to expire quietly and unnoticed.

The responsibilty of universities

A canvass of the law brings us to the final and in many ways the most compelling objection to speech codes. Apart from legality and practicality, growing numbers of observers ask whether a university has any business banning certain messages. Of course there are limits on campus speech. If a student cheats on an exam or plagiarizes a paper and is threatened with dismissal, there will be little point in reminding the dean or committee that the act involved speech. Or if a student in a foreign language course gets a lower grade because a forbidden English translation of the major work has been used during a test, there is little solicitude for the student's undoubted right in any other context to read freely. In these and other situations, much like criminal conspiracies and solicitations under the general law, speech is being punished—but clearly not because of its message or viewpoint. Such easy cases do not help much in addressing the far harder question of curbing racist, sexist, and ethnically demeaning campus speech.

The central premise behind most speech codes is that certain messages are so harmful or so at variance with the goals of higher education that they do not belong on a college campus. Senior members of the academic community have heard this argument before. In the 1950s it took two ominous forms. One related to communist or "fellow traveler" professors whose views were said to be so dangerous and so antithetical to free and open inquiry that their presence on the faculty and in the classroom could no longer be tolerated. Sadly, some of the nation's preeminent universities acceded to such pressures and dismissed politically unorthodox scholars, sometimes on the pretext that they had refused to cooperate with legislative committees, but at heart because of their "dangerous" or "inimical" views.

During the same period, the nation encountered the issue in a quite different form. Some states adopted speaker bans, the effect of which was to bar communists and others of suspect views from appearing on public campuses in these states. Repealing such laws, even after they had out-lived their usefulness, was politically risky. Only occasionally could judges be persuaded to set them aside on free speech grounds. Most per-suasive was an argument that has been surprisingly little used in the speech code context: if a university bars one idea or viewpoint from the campus, it implicitly endorses all others. The only safe way to avoid such an inference of approval is to bar nothing and thus endorse nothing. So it is with speech codes: if the university is in the business of excluding or punishing certain messages or viewpoints, it is difficult to avoid implying that everything else has been officially approved. And such an impri-matur is precisely what U.S. universities have sought to avoid—at least since Thomas Jefferson established a university where error is permitted "so long as reason is free to pursue it . . ."

There is, moreover, a certain arrogance in assuming the capacity to determine what is "right" and what is "wrong" for campus consumption. Former Harvard president Derek Bok, a vigorous and consistent critic of such rules, asked:

> Whom will we trust to censor communications and decide which ones are "too offensive" or "too inflammatory" or too devoid of intellectual content? . . . As a former President of the University of California once said: "The University is not engaged in making ideas safe for students. It is engaged in making students safe for ideas."

There is a fundamental dissonance between controlling words and the very nature of a university as a place of free inquiry. Consider care-fully the sort of example a college or university sets for its students by de-claring officially that certain thoughts or viewpoints—however hateful and repugnant—are off-limits on its campus. Efforts to excise or punish abhorrent views imply that the normal modes of academic discourse—reason and persuasion—have failed, so that prohibition becomes by de-fault the only viable option. The 1992 statement of Committee A of the American Association of University Professors, On *Freedom of Expression and Campus Speech Codes*, captures the point well:

> By proscribing any ideas, a university sets an example that profoundly disserves its academic mission. . . . [A] college or university sets a perilous course if it seeks to differentiate be-tween high-value and low-value speech, or to choose which groups are to be protected by curbing the speech of others. A speech code unavoidably implies an institutional compe-tence to distinguish permissible expression of hateful thought from what is to be proscribed as thoughtless hate.

9

The Popular Culture Industry Should Censor Itself

William Baldwin, Peter Bart, Michael Bay, Stephen Collins, Chuck D, Amitai Etzioni, and Arianna Huffington

William Baldwin is an actor and the president of the First Amendment advocacy group Creative Coalition; Peter Bart is the editor-in-chief of Variety; *Michael Bay is a film director; Stephen Collins is an actor and founding member of the Creative Coalition; Chuck D is a rap artist and Creative Coalition advisory board member; Amitai Etzioni is the director of the Institute for Communitarian Policy Studies; Arianna Huffington is a syndicated columnist.*

The movie, television, and video game industries should be more willing to self-censor their products' violent content because the First Amendment should not be used to validate offensive material. While purveyors of popular culture have the right to create what they wish, these industries ought to think of how they affect their viewers, especially children, when they make violence seem like an ordinary and pervasive part of life. In addition, parents need to take an active role in controlling what their children are exposed to. With the help of government regulations on advertising content, and media establishment of a realistic guidance system, parents will be better able to protect their children.

WILLIAM BALDWIN: We're in a unique position in the entertainment industry. We have—for some strange and probably unhealthy reason—a disproportionate amount of access and opportunity and empowerment and influence. What the Creative Coalition wants to do is recognize this disturbing fact . . . and utilize it as constructively and as responsibly as we possibly can.

PETER BART: So, here's the problem: Everyone is opposed to violence in the media; essentially no one agrees to the causes and remedies. In reading up for this, I've written down a few quick factoids, which I'll relate very quickly. The average 12-year-old has seen 8,000 murders and 100,000 acts of violence on TV by the time he hits 12, but no one knows to what effect. CBS, the geezer network, has three times as much violence as NBC, but no one knows why and the PAX network has no violence at all except that done for plot and character development. Criminals like to blame things on movies. Tim McVeigh said that seeing a movie called *Red Dawn* caused him to blow up Oklahoma [City]. . . . All of which leads us to inquire: What the hell can we do about it? Arianna, if I can pick on you first, we've got the FCC invading this domain. You've got the surgeon general, maybe the Senate's cultural warriors. Is there really a role for government to play in this arena?

Strengthening civic virtue

ARIANNA HUFFINGTON: There is a tremendous role for the bully pulpit and that's what I think has been missing. We've tried to pick apart and point fingers to compartmentalize where the problems lie, and we've missed the thing that for me is the most important issue. And this is that as a society we have become so atomized, so concerned about seeing everything purely in terms of economic self-interest, that we have really pushed aside what the founding of this country has been about. . . .

I think that the founding principle of America, and something we've gotten away from, is about the public good and not just the individual pursuit of our own happiness. In fact, when the Founding Fathers talked about the pursuit of happiness, there had been a debate as to if they should have mentioned virtue instead of happiness. It was much deeper and it was much more about civic participation and feeling good by doing good than we have kind of allowed it to degenerate to. . . . This is not accomplished through legislation but through a constant process of recognizing that a society cannot survive—a civilization cannot survive—without the civic virtue, which has to be strengthened at every turn.

PB: But can civic virtue be strengthened when you talk about violence, about violence in movies and television? I mean, if you turn on the local news, it seems to me you see a cavalcade of violence hour after hour. Michael, as a director . . . does this get to you?

MICHAEL BAY: You know, I don't really watch local news because the first ten minutes is a murder count. And I think there's something to be said [for the fact] that there's such a big status of celebrity-ism in America that viewers who see these murderers, they go out and they do something to get validated. They do something very socially unacceptable. There's a telling little tale that I heard from the kid who killed three kids after he was watching *Dune*; after Columbine happened he said, "God, I'm gonna be yesterday's news." And that really just hit me—it was like, wow, this poor country is in trouble.

Re-educating the news media

STEPHEN COLLINS: There's a wonderful mathematician and writer named John Allen Paulos who writes a lot about the news and math—and he writes for lay people so I can understand it. He pointed out exactly what you're talking about, Michael, which is that over the last 15 or 20 years all the rules about what is acceptable, newsworthy news on television has changed. It happened precisely at the moment when 24-hour news became a reality, and news inevitably had to become software, it had to become entertainment. And by definition, if you're showing 24-hour news, you can't show the same story 3 hours in a row. The story has to change even if the story doesn't change. One of the things that started happening was they realized that crisis and murder and mayhem spiked the ratings. . . .

[Paulos] said that the trick that's played on the public is that one-third of the news is about violence, and the public, over time, starts to say, "Gee, that's a third of what's happening out there." Now the fact is, per capita violence has not risen appreciably in this century. It's probably declined. So you have this perception out there that we're a more violent society and a more dangerous world. When Johnny Carson started doing monologues about New York City in the '70s, I had a friend in Minneapolis who said to me, "Now you live in New York: How do you go to the supermarket? What do you do?" He actually sort of imagined me dodging bullets. There is a very real perception that the news is creating. You couple it with a culture of celebrity where if you're not beautiful, a sports hero, a political hero, or an artist, what chance do you have to get famous? Well, you can pick up a gun and get famous real fast.

The average 12-year-old has seen 8,000 murders and 100,000 acts of violence on TV by the time he hits 12.

I think one of the things we have to do is re-educate news editors as to what is newsworthy. And it's scarier now because there's really four news outlets: there's Rupert Murdoch, there's Time Warner, there's Viacom, and there's Disney. We get all our news from them now, and they now exert a tremendous amount of control on the local level because those are all their affiliates.

PB: And as an editor, I wouldn't hold out much hope for educating editors.

SC: I don't hold out a lot of hope either. But you know, television did a complete turn around on smoking. Forty years ago television glorified smoking and sold it avidly to the American public. Once the studies came and people realized what it was meaning in their lives, television was able to turn it around just as they've turned around sexual and racial stereotypes in a huge way. I think television has a great capacity to make both news and art stories tell tales that glorify nonviolence as opposed to violence.

The powers of the First Amendment

PB: Dr. Etzioni, since you have written 60 [*sic*] books in this area, could you explicate? Whenever we have discussions about what can be done, we run into people saying the First Amendment protects and also punishes.

AMITAI ETZIONI: Sure. Let me first say the First Amendment will not protect those of you who make this stuff. The reason is very simple. The

First Amendment allows you to do things, but it doesn't make them right. It gives you the legal title to say practically any horrible thing you can imagine. I can say, under my right to free speech, that all the homeless people should be shot, or all the Jews, or all black people—all kinds of horrible things. Doesn't make them right.

So the question we're talking about is not is there some legalism behind which you can protect yourself, but how you look at yourself in the mirror in the morning. What are you going to tell your children, what are you going to tell your friends, what do you want written in your obituary? Do you want to say that you made more money than anyone else, or do you want to say that there is something decent in all of us? And so the question is: Are we going to build on that and push the envelope in some other way than we are now?

The First Amendment allows you to do things, but it doesn't make them right.

When President Reagan was chiding the creative community for glorifying drugs, it protested, shouting "First Amendment, First Amendment!"—then it corrected itself to some extent. Stereotypes have not disappeared. But I don't think anybody today would make the kind of movies they used to make about African-Americans, or even about Africa, as you see in *Tarzan*. Gay relationships are dealt with not perfectly and openly, but much better. So there is a long way to go. But if just a little more is done for those of us who are concerned about family, decency, and relationships which are not money-based, we'll be home free.

PB: Where I still get lost, and help me on this, is what do we do about it then? Does the market system correct itself as you [Etzioni] suggest?

CHUCK D: . . . A guy that's in charge of a supercorporation that might spew out movies that might be derogatory to a certain makeup of people—he's looking at his P's and Q's, sitting around a table with his lawyers and his accountants, and the only thing he gives a damn about is that bottom line. . . . And who is this guy? And what is his Social Security number and where does he live and what Town Car does he get in when he leaves his house and goes to work? We just would like to know [for] when he happens to put out something and feels unaccountable to the communities that he's putting it out in front of. It's like when you turn on a light switch, and you happen to have roaches in your house, they start scrambling and whatever . . . same thing with the heads of these supercorporations, whether it be film, whether it be movies, whether it be the head of the news. . . . I don't think these culprits are being identified enough.

The media and advertising

SC: I think there is such a fear—in our business particularly—of being unhip and uncool. For instance, they say the definition of a conservative is a liberal with a teenage daughter. I have an almost-10-year-old daughter and so I watch a lot of Nickelodeon in my house. And I am appalled at how you know if a commercial is a boy ad or a girl ad. The girl ads are all "dee dee dee dee" and the boy ads are all "storm-and-killer-gonna-come-get-you!" Every single one. There are no gray areas. I'm talking Nickelodeon here. I think someone has to take advertisers to task. It takes people—it probably takes people like us in large groups or people who are seen to be moneymakers—to go in and say to advertisers, "Stop doing this." Because, as you [Etzioni] were saying, it is ultimately a matter of personal conscience. The government can't censor it. You can do all the movie ratings you want, people individually have to start waking up to the fruits of what they're doing.

PB: But guys, don't you think that as the media consolidations grow, as the companies get bigger and bigger, you get involved with corporations that are really more like nation-states, which are essentially insensitive to any pressures of this sort? You can't identify an individual to follow home, you have to follow a committee. I wonder whether or not we're being unrealistic about our efforts to deal with companies on this sort of reasonable basis. Do you agree?

AH: . . . [T]he system is just incredibly interconnected. Corporations and the violence that's produced and the two-tiered justice and everything is very connected to our political system because these corporations are the biggest contributors to our campaign finance system. It's all like one big blob. And we have to sort of calculate from all different aspects. And we have to do it soon and that's why we cannot waste the year 2000 as an opportunity for leadership because we need the megaphone.

I love the slogan of the Creative Coalition about using the voice you are given because some people are just opting out of the system. And especially the young—they're opting out politically. Fewer and fewer are voting. They are really feeling so disempowered. In the last tally done by Michigan University [*sic*] that tracks these trends, 65 percent of Americans believe that our government is run by special interests and there is nothing they can do about it. So, it will take sort of everything we have, and it will take a sort of urgency: if we don't all get involved, things are only going to get worse.

Parental responsibility

CD: The video game industry is just off the hook. People know already how it feels to blow blood out of somebody's skull because they do it repeatedly, day after day after day. And the leaders of that industry just go off and live in Bel Air. They go to their refrigerator and get a nice glass of iced tea and, you know, hug their family real close and hope their kids don't fall victim to the same programming that they put out there.

I think, like Stephen said, if hip is here, and hip gets you $10, but intelligent might get you $9, it's the whole process of big business of more more more, get get get, greed greed greed, by any means necessary. . . . It's just like how many people will settle for the 9 and just say, "I'm not going to go for the 10. Let some idiot go for the 10."

Like Stephen, I have an 11-year-old daughter, 7-year-old daughter, 13-year-old son to raise. Raising a child [today] is synonymous with programming—but to program your child, you've [first] got to deprogram. You have got to empty the trash like you do on the computer and reprogram.

PB: Let me just try to see where we are in place here. You certainly made a persuasive point in that it does boil down to parental responsibility . . .

AE: The phrase "it comes down to parental responsibility" could be understood to mean that that's where it begins and ends. So if parents would just turn off the television set, then the whole problem would go away. I don't think that's quite the way the data takes us. First of all, parents cannot control the media all by themselves. We need a realistic guidance system so they can tell what's there; otherwise, they will have to watch all those programs to be able to tell what they are supposed to protect their children from. Second, unless we stop sending them both to work outside the household, we have about 10 million children coming home—the latchkey children—where there is no parent at home. If it "all ends with parents' responsibility," the media could escape responsibility.

SC: I think that there's a need for some kind of regulation on advertising. What's happening right at this moment—everyone knows we're in a teen wave in this culture. What we've done is we've figured out, massively figured out, how to market to teens. We know how to do that. What we've done is we're preparing teens to be nothing more than teens. Culture gives teens exactly what they know teens want, and they don't for a second try to give a teen anything that a teen wouldn't want. So we're abdicating any sort of moral stance in entertainment; we're feeding them because we figured out what they want. It's like giving chocolate to a chocoholic: they'll take it all day. Advertisers have got to sit down and realize that the dollars they're putting behind programming are having this effect in the culture.

WB: Doctor, you made an interesting comment before about the media escaping responsibility. I do think, you know, in 1965, pregnant women did not realize that smoking caused any kind of fetal damage. It seems strange 30 years later—how could they not know that? I think we're at the same point with media violence now; I think clearly we know there is mounting evidence . . . media violence isn't the cause of violence—but it's a contributing factor. And guns are a contributing factor, and poverty is a contributing factor, and broken homes, and double income families, and racial diversity, ethnic diversity—all could be possible contributing factors to violence. My question to you is: What do you think are some of the other underlying social causes for violence in our culture?

AE: There is no question that guns account for much more of the problem than all of the other factors together. Even if you were to eliminate poverty and purify the media, you still would have a major problem unless you did something with the guns. But there is no way to have a perfect social system. If we say we're going to eradicate illness or environmental problems, all we can do is try to make partial, incremental improvements. So what we want from the media is to do its share, realizing that even if they do it to perfection, the problem will not go away—we're just going to save 22 percent more lives.

The tradition that I'm coming from says that if you save one life, it's like you saved the whole world—so let's do that, let's save one life at a time. And the way to do that, I think, as Stephen said a moment ago, is to have some minimum standards. We're going to have to tell each other, "OK, you want to make money and you want to push the envelope. But at some point, if you want to belong to a decent community, you can't go there."

10

Popular Culture Should Not Be Censored

John Derbyshire

John Derbyshire is a novelist and contributing editor to National Review.

Although it may seem unsavory at times, popular culture does not pose a threat to children and should not be censored. Parents have a greater influence on children than do fictional violence or songs with adult themes. Seeking to restrict the content of popular media, through regulations or moral crusades, is unnecessary and could lead to additional efforts to weaken the First Amendment.

On September 9, 2000, we had our annual block party in my suburban, lower-middle-class street. The event's centerpiece was a talent show, the brainchild of our 10-year-old neighbor Siobhan. She herself performed three songs: "It Was Our Day," from the group B*Witched, and the Britney Spears numbers "What U See (Is What U Get)" and "Lucky."

Sex, death, and popular culture

For readers not au courant with the pop-music scene, the first of these songs is a mawkish elegy for a dead friend: "Heaven, heaven was calling you/Heaven, heaven needed you/I'll lay a rose beside you for ever." The second is a girl's protest against her boyfriend's possessiveness: "I know you watch me when I'm dancin'/When I party with my friends/I can feel your eyes on my back, baby/I can't have no chains around me." The third is about the inner loneliness of a Hollywood star: "She's so lucky, she's a star/But she cry, cry, cries in her lonely heart."

So there I was, sitting on a plastic chair on my neighbor's lawn, watching a 10-year-old girl singing about grief, sexual jealousy, and the hollowness of success. As I squirmed, I sank into reflections of the curmudgeonly kind: Is this all kids know nowadays? There used to be innocent songs that preteens could sing—I can remember a hundred of them: "Green Grow the Rushes-O" and so on. Now there are no topics, for anyone of any age, but sex and death. Miss Spears had been in the newspapers that very morning; at the MTV Music Video Awards two nights before, 18-year-old Britney had taken off everything but a few strategic spangles and performed the kind of dance for which lonely men in soiled raincoats used to pay extravagant door charges to ill-lit basement clubs. If I were to tell you that I switched the thing off in disgust I should be guilty of a falsehood; but I am awfully glad my daughter Nellie (a 7-year-old whose contribution to the talent show was a faultless performance of Dvorak's "Humoresque" on violin) didn't see it. Yet even she already knows some Britney lyrics. They all do, preteens and pre-preteens. As parents say with a sigh, when you bring this up: It's the culture.

The culture came up often over the next few days. The following Monday the Federal Trade Commission (FTC) released its report on the marketing of violence in the media. Meanwhile, the Senate Commerce Committee was holding hearings on the issue. Lynne Cheney showed up to urge show business to police itself, and to quote some lyrics from hip-hop star Eminem, who had won a major award at the MTV bash. One of Eminem's songs expresses the satisfaction a man feels at having raped and murdered his mother. Joe Lieberman went further before the committee, urging the FTC to step in and regulate media companies who would not tone down their products. Al Gore, on his way from one show-biz fund-raiser ($800,000) to another ($6.5 million), agreed.

Three approaches to regulation

What to make of all this? So far as public policy is concerned, there are three possible positions, identified here by those who take them.

My neighbors: It doesn't matter much, so there's no point getting steamed. As an influence on the development of my children, my words and my example outweigh by a factor of hundreds anything Britney Spears does.

Mrs. Cheney: The media companies that promote creatures like Eminem should be shamed before the public, and thereby persuaded to mend their ways. Gore-Lieberman and their trial-lawyer pals: Legislate, regulate, intimidate. Sure, there'll be some grumbling from Hollywood; but they will never defect to the party of the dreaded "Christian Right."

Most conservatives would sympathize with Mrs. Cheney; I greatly admire her myself. If, however, my neighbors are representative of the larger American public, as they probably are, then her program is a non-starter. We must therefore choose between the first of the above options and the third. Can there be any doubt which poses the greater threat to our ancient liberties?

What we are talking about here, remember, is sex and violence. The second of these gives me no trouble. I have never had much patience with the idea that children should be shielded from fictional violence. I would much rather my own children discover *The Hunchback of Notre Dame* as I did, in the thrilling sado-necrophiliac original, shot through with cruelty and lust, than via the lame jollity of the Disney version. Here I can appeal to the wisdom of great storytellers from the past, who spared children very little. Check out the original "Cinderella," in which the ugly sisters get their eyes pecked out. Children take this stuff in their stride. They may even, as [psychologist] Bruno Bettelheim argued, be helped by it.

Certainly the evidence that exposure to graphic violence causes violent deeds is highly suspect: "Shooting the Messenger," a recent report by the Media Coalition (available on their website), persuasively refutes the kiddie-see, kiddie-do arguments.

Popular culture is not dangerous

Sex is more worrisome. As the doting father of little Nellie, I naturally spend a lot of time fretting about this. How will the vulgarity of our public entertainment shape her personality? Our September 9 block party came on the anniversary of Elvis Presley's first appearance on the *Ed Sullivan Show* 44 years ago. The following January, Sullivan had Elvis on for the third time; it was then that he issued his famous order for the singer to be shown only from the waist up, in order that younger viewers might not be inflamed by the sight of his hip movement. We have traveled an awfully long way from Ed Sullivan to the MTV awards show. What is really surprising, though, is how little harm has been done. It needs some effort of imagination now to recall the alarm that Elvis raised at that time. Frank Sinatra called Elvis's music "the most brutal, ugly, desperate, vicious form of expression it has been my misfortune to hear." This comment reflected a widespread public attitude.

If, in 1956, you had asked any thoughtful American what consequences might follow from the abandonment of all customary restraint in entertainment, and from related phenomena like the attempted normalization of homosexuality, he would probably have said that the Republic could not survive such a transformation. Plainly these good people believed something that was, in fact, untrue: that the stability of society depended on the exclusion, by common consent, of certain things from the sphere of public display.

The insouciance of my neighbors in the face of today's popular culture is, therefore, quite sensible. It's the culture—but it doesn't matter; it does no great harm.

To be sure, much mayhem has passed before our eyes since 1956. We have gone through Francis Fukuyama's "great disruption" with all its attendant phenomena: soaring rates of crime, bastardy, divorce, and so on. But we have come through to the other side at last; as Fukuyama himself points out, the indicators are trending downwards now, toward "renormalization." And in all that happened, which was cause and which effect? Did Elvis—or Madonna, or Howard Stern—have one-thousandth the influence on our culture that (say) the Pill had?

The world changes. As a conservative, I shall conserve what I can; but if I am to keep any influence over my children at all, some measured degree of acceptance is called for. There is a price to be paid for liberty, and Eminem and Britney Spears are the current coin in which that price must be paid. They will not be shamed, and they ought not be banned: for if the guardians of our public virtue can outlaw hip-hop lyrics, you can be sure that "hate speech" will be their next target, and it is all too easy to imagine where that will lead. With the Second Amendment swirling down the drain, the survival of the First can no longer be taken for granted.

11

Limited Restrictions on Internet Hate Speech May Be Necessary

Laura Leets

Laura Leets is an assistant professor of communications at Stanford University in Palo Alto, California.

Very limited restrictions of hate speech on the Internet should be considered because such speech can have serious short-term and long-term consequences. Among the effects of hate speech is the encouragement of racist and sexist beliefs that can culminate in violence. However, it may be difficult to determine how best to regulate hate expression on the Internet because cyberspace has no geographic boundaries; laws that are valid in one state or nation may be unenforceable elsewhere.

There's been a groundswell [since the late 1990s] to increase diversity in journalism, both in news coverage and in newsroom staffing. The goal of several diversity initiatives is to increase the number of voices that regularly appear in our newspapers, magazines, broadcasts and Web sites.

It's important to seek different perspectives and ideas, and the goal of such initiatives is an admirable and productive one. There are some voices, however, that have demonstrably adverse effects. So while the journalism community, judicial system and American public generally support tolerance of diverse viewpoints, some perspectives and types of speech still warrant concern.

The rise in hate crimes

One problematic voice is that of hate. Whether it is the dragging death of an African-American behind a pick-up truck in Texas, a gay student's murder in Wyoming, a racially motivated shooting spree at a Los Angeles Jewish community center or a bloody rampage by two high school students enamored of Adolf Hitler's fascism, the rising incidence of hate crimes and the groups who appear to encourage them is attracting public interest. In particular, the World Wide Web has provided marginalized extremist groups a more notable and accessible public platform. The Internet has put the problem of incendiary hate into sharp relief.

In several research studies where I have focused on short-term message effects of hate speech, it is difficult to demonstrate with certainty the linkage between hate expression and violence or harm (deterministic causality). In one study, I asked 266 participants (both university and non-university students recruited online) to read and evaluate one of 11 white supremacist Web pages that I had randomly sampled from the Internet. Similar to previous studies, the data showed that the content of the hate Web pages was perceived to be in keeping with the Court bounds for First Amendment protection. Yet the participants acknowledged an indirect effect that, on the other hand, may suggest hate speech effects are more slow-acting—and thus imperceptible in the short term (probabilistic causality).

Specifically, participants in the cyberhate study rated the indirect threats from [the white supremacy group] the World Church of the Creator (WCOTC) Web page as very high (Mean=6, on a seven-point scale where seven represented the highest score). Is it coincidental that a former WCOTC member recently shot 11 Asian-Americans, African-Americans and Jews, killing two, before committing suicide? Or that two brothers associated with WCOTC were charged with murdering a gay couple and firebombing three Sacramento synagogues? While WCOTC leader Matthew Hale does not endorse this lawlessness, neither does he condemn it. Part of their ideology is that all nonwhites are "mud people," people without souls, like animals eligible for harm.

Current legal remedies may be missing the real harm of racist indoctrination, which may not be immediately apparent or verifiable. For instance, hate expressions tend to encourage a set of beliefs that develop gradually and that often can lie dormant until conditions are ripe for a climate of moral exclusion and subsequent crimes against humanity. Moral exclusion is defined by Susan Opotow, an independent scholar affiliated with Teachers College at Columbia University, as the psychosocial orientation toward individuals or groups for whom justice principles or considerations of fairness are not applicable. People who are morally excluded are perceived as nonentities, and harming them appears acceptable and just (e.g., slavery, holocaust).

It is not the abstract viewpoints that are problematic. Rather, it is the expressions intending to elicit persecution or oppression that often begin with dehumanizing rhetoric. In my research, I argue that communication is the primary means by which psychological distancing occurs. Arguably, it may be the long-term, not short-term, effects of hate expression that are potentially more far reaching.

Understanding Internet law

Even though prevailing First Amendment dogma maintains that speech may not be penalized merely because its content is racist, sexist or basically abhorrent, Internet law is a dynamic area and as such is not completely integrated into our regulatory and legal system. Consequently, many questions remain about how traditional laws should apply to this new and unique medium.

The Internet can combine elements of print (newspapers and magazines), broadcast (television and radio) and face-to-face interaction. Moreover, unlike users of previous media, those on the Internet have the power to reach a mass audience, but in this case the audience must be more active in seeking information, as cyberspace is less intrusive than other mass media.

It may be the long-term, not short-term, effects of hate expression that are potentially more far reaching.

It is unclear whether content-based restrictions found in other technological media may be permissible for the Internet. For example, the Federal Communications Commission (FCC) ruled that indecency was unsuitable for broadcast media because of ease of access, invasiveness and spectrum scarcity, yet cable and print media are not subjected to this form of content regulation.

In 1996, the United States Congress passed the Telecommunications Bill, which included the Communications Decency Act (CDA). The CDA regulated indecent or obscene material for adults on the Internet, applying First Amendment jurisprudence from broadcast and obscenity cases. Later that year, the Supreme Court declared two provisions unconstitutional in *Reno vs. ACLU*. Congress and the Court disagreed on the medium-specific constitutional speech standard suitable for the World Wide Web. Congress argued that the Internet should be regulated in the same manner as television or radio, but the Court decided not to apply that doctrinal framework. Instead, the Court viewed the Internet as face-to-face communication, deserving full protection.

Issues of Internet regulation naturally lead to the question of whether such regulation is even possible. Cyberspace doesn't have geographical boundaries, so it is difficult to determine where violations of the law should be prosecuted. There are enforcement conflicts, not only between different countries' legal jurisdictions, but also among federal, state and local levels in the United States. Although Americans place a high premium on free expression, without much effort most people can find Internet material that they would want to censor.

Cause and effect

Some argue that cyberhate oversteps this idea of "mere insult" and warrants liability. The Internet is a powerful forum of communication with its broad (world-wide) reach, interactivity and multi-media capability to disseminate information. These features inevitably result in concerns about impact, especially when viewed as empowering racists and other extremists. It is common for people to wonder whether white supremacist Web pages cause hate crime. This question is similar to people's concerns regarding whether TV violence causes aggression in viewers. The issue of causation (claim: x causes y) is an important one to address.

It is important to differentiate between language determining (or causing) an effect and language influencing the probability of an effect. In terms of a strict social science approach (deterministic causation) we can't say language has an effect unless three conditions are met: (a) there must be a relationship between the hypothesized cause and the observed effect, (b) the cause must always precede the effect in time (x must come before y), and (c) all alternative explanations for the effect must be eliminated. The problem with making a strong case for a causal effect lies with the second and third conditions. For example, most media (television, Internet etc.) effects are probabilistic, not deterministic. It is almost impossible to make a clear case for television or cyberhate effects because the relationship is almost never a simple causal one. Instead, there are many factors in the influence process. Each factor increases the probability of an effect occurring. The effects process is complex.

The U.S. Supreme Court has traditionally viewed speech effects in terms of short-term, deterministic consequences, and has not considered more far-reaching effects.

While more research is needed on the long-term effects of hate speech, it may be worth considering some very limited restrictions on some hate expression. American jurisprudence has not fully realized the harmful nature and effects stemming from hate speech, which has the ability both to directly elicit immediate behavior (short term) and to cultivate an oppressive climate (long term).

12

Freedom of Speech Can Prevent Hate Crimes

Aryeh Neier

Aryeh Neier is the president of the Open Society Institute in New York, which provides financial, technical, and administrative support for the Soros Foundation, a collection of nonprofit foundations located throughout the world.

A request by Nazis to march in Skokie, Illinois, a Rwandan radio station's encouragement of genocide, and Serbian media's fomenting of ethnic cleansing are three situations that can help clarify the relationship between free expression and hate speech. In the case of the Nazis, their hate speech should be protected because it could do little harm; in fact, such a demonstration by a minority group would likely be met by widespread protest that would actually facilitate dialogue about such views. In contrast, Rwandan radio station Mille Collines and the Serbian state television and radio network were able to incite violence because they monopolized communication and silenced dissident views. The Rwandan and Serbian tragedies illustrate that freedom of speech is the best way to prevent hate crimes.

In 1977, I helped to defend freedom of speech for a group of American Nazis. There was nothing particularly unusual in this: the American Civil Liberties Union has frequently defended Nazis, members of the Ku Klux Klan and others engaged in hate speech. Yet it aroused great controversy because of the drama of the situation: the Nazis wished to march through Skokie, Illinois, a town with a large population of Holocaust survivors. I thought then, and think now, that it was important to protect free expression even for such a repugnant group.

Free expression versus hate speech

Two cases that could be considered by UN Security Council tribunals—the prosecution of those who incited genocide on Radio Mille Collines in

From "Clear and Present Danger," by Aryeh Neier, *Index on Censorship*, 1998. Copyright © 1998 by *Index on Censorship*. Reprinted with permission.

Rwanda and those who fomented ethnic cleansing through the Serbian media—may appear to raise some of the same issues as the Skokie case. But in the Rwandan case, and perhaps also in the Serbian one, I find myself on the opposite side. Comparing these three situations might help to clarify some of the issues around the vexed problem of free expression and hate speech.

It is vital to defend freedom of speech even in unpleasant circumstances.

The Skokie case arose in the 1970s because a small group of US Nazis was trying to exploit a tense racial situation in Chicago. In Marquette Park, which divided a white working-class neighbourhood from a predominantly black one, the Martin Luther King Junior Coalition was holding demonstrations calling for desegregation. The Nazi group rented a store-front next to the park and started to organise counter-protests. Concerned about the possibility of open conflict, the Chicago authorities demanded that the Nazis post a bond of US$250,000 to repair any damage that might result—a typical ploy then used by US city authorities to restrict free speech and assembly for despised groups. The local office of the ACLU agreed to challenge the bond requirement, but while the lawsuit was under way, the Nazi group was shut out of Marquette Park.

Searching for a way to keep itself in the public eye, the group sent letters to all the suburban communities and towns near Chicago asking to hold demonstrations there. Most of them wisely ignored the request, but Skokie responded with an angry refusal and quickly adopted a series of ordinances forbidding marches with Nazi symbols and repeating the city of Chicago's bond requirement. The Nazi group again came to the ACLU—which takes every case brought to it where it believes freedom of speech is at stake—to ask for representation. The ACLU agreed to file a lawsuit against the town of Skokie.

During the debate that raged nationwide throughout the 15 months of a series of court cases, many people argued that the Nazis should not be allowed to march. Some drew on the doctrine of 'clear and present danger', which the US Supreme Court had invoked on a number of occasions to limit freedom of speech. The doctrine of 'clear and present danger' stems from the period after World War I which saw some 1,900 federal prosecutions for peaceful speech, mostly for statements considered subversive because they encouraged resistance to the draft or otherwise opposed the war effort. Among the notable cases of that era was the prosecution and imprisonment of the leader of the American Socialist Party, Eugene V. Debs, which was upheld by the Supreme Court. The restrictive force of the doctrine was broadened in 1951 during the prosecution of 11 top US Communist Party leaders, when the Supreme Court ruled that if the climate is right for an evil to occur, the government may imprison people whose advocacy could create that evil at a future point. If the Supreme Court had adhered to this view, which it subsequently abandoned, the government would have had a powerful tool to crack down on all manner of speech that particular officials might find offensive.

The dangers of one point of view

Now contrast the circumstances of the Nazis in Skokie, the anti-war protesters during World War I and the US Communists in the early 1950s with that of the hate broadcasters in Rwanda and Serbia. In the US cases, the groups whose free speech was at issue were minorities representing dissenting points of view. Even if the deeds they advocated were unlawful, everyone had an opportunity to hear contrary views before any crime was committed. Indeed, opposing points of view all but drowned out these minorities. Defending them protected freedom of speech. There was no manifest danger that the violence they might incite would follow so soon that debate could not take place. That is, the danger was neither clear nor present.

In Rwanda, on the other hand, Radio Mille Collines had virtually a monopoly for its hate-filled broadcasts. No contrary view had a chance to be heard. Moreover, once the genocide started, Radio Mille Collines took over the task of organising it, directing mobs and militias to the places where the Tutsi targets were taking shelter. The violence that was incited was inextricably linked to its broadcasts. Circumstances in Serbia were not quite so extreme, but they were similar. The state television and radio network, RTS, had a monopoly on broadcasting and used it to stir up hate and to mobilise violence.

The Rwandan and Serbian cases show why it is vital to defend freedom of speech even in unpleasant circumstances, as the ACLU did in Skokie. The reason the media were so effective in inciting violence in Rwanda and Yugoslavia is precisely that they had an exclusive capacity to communicate. If a variety of views were being expressed and heard in Rwanda, even the vilest radio station could not have incited a genocide in which 800,000 people were killed during a period of three months. If there had been an opportunity for other voices to be heard in Serbia in the period when RTS and the nationalist press were monopolising communication, the influence of those voices would not have been so extreme. Freedom of speech is ultimately the greatest protection against the kinds of crimes that took place in Rwanda and in the former Yugoslavia, and against the crimes that [anti-Semitic publisher] Julius Streicher was able to incite in Nazi Germany. It is the exclusive capacity to communicate that produces the link between incitement to violence and violence itself.

13

Flag Burning Should Be Banned

Patrick Brady

Patrick Brady, a retired army major general, is a winner of the Congressional Medal of Honor and the chairman of the Citizens' Flag Alliance, a coalition of organizations that encourages Congress to pass a constitutional amendment that will ban flag desecration.

A constitutional amendment banning flag burning and other types of flag desecration should be passed. Contrary to Supreme Court rulings and the opinion of people who oppose such an amendment, flag burning is not a form of speech. The flag desecration amendment has widespread public support, would restore the Constitution to its original meaning, and would help instill patriotism.

The enemy today is more formidable than any of you [members of the military organization the American Legion] faced on the battlefield. The debate in the House on the flag highlighted the great divide in our nation on the Constitution and the very definition of patriotism. Our opposition defines the essence of freedom as the toleration of unpatriotic conduct.

They actually separate our freedoms from patriotism and have their own version of patriotism. And they separate our laws from our values. They say the flag symbolizes the freedom to burn it; that our flag is the symbol of un-patriotic conduct. That burning the symbol of patriotism is patriotic.

They cower before the courts, they believe the courts not "WE THE PEOPLE" rule. And for good reason. Many of them know that their agenda could never survive in the bright lights of the public square, where the people rule. Their only hope is in the courtroom where the dark robed un-elected elite rule.

In the hostility of the media environment in which we all live, sound bites are the norm. It is true that if one can control the language, control of minds is not far behind. In a few seconds opinion is formed and laws are made. Tragically, many sound bites are false and misleading and we are led astray.

Excerpted from Patrick Brady's remarks delivered at the American Legion 83rd Annual National Convention in San Antonio, Texas, August 28, 2001. Copyright © 2001 by Patrick Brady. Reprinted with permission.

Flag burning is not speech

For this reason it is vital that we fill our quiver with truth bites as we go into battle with those who would disfigure America and teach our children flag desecration is speech. We must out communicate them. We cannot repeat too often these truths.

Never forget that the foundation of all we are doing for the flag is the Constitution. The Constitution is the foundation of all we are and the only guarantee of our future. It is under attack and little understood by too many of our people.

To those who say that burning the flag is speech, ask what is said when the flag is burned. Ask how you burn a flag with your tongue. [Former baseball manager] Tommy Lasorda said that speech is when you talk. Our opponents believe they are wiser than 80% of the people, 70% of the Congress, 4 Chief Justices of the United States as well as Justices on 5 other Supreme Courts in the last century who agree with Tommy.

If they disagree with this mighty armada of flag defenders ask them if they also disagree with James Madison, who wrote the First Amendment, and Thomas Jefferson who also agree with Tommy. [Representative] Richard Gephardt, Missouri, was right in condemning those who seek to distort our Constitution while cloaking themselves in a disguise of free speech.

To those who say the flag is precious to them but the Constitution is more precious, ask if they have any possession that is precious to them, any one or anything that they love, that they would not protect. Pat Boone compared this to saying that he loved his mother but it was okay to bat her around.

If they say they do not want to amend the Constitution for the flag tell them that we are not amending the Constitution for the flag, we are doing it for the Constitution.

Refuting the arguments

To those who worry about making felons of flag burners, tell them we oppose that. Tell them that flag burners are not the problem; the problem is those who distort our Constitution by calling flag burning speech.

To all who find virtue in bashing our values, who say we must tolerate conduct that the majority find offensive or evil, ask where that is written in the Constitution.

If anyone says this amendment damages the constitution, read the amendment to them and remind them that it damages nothing because it changes nothing; it simply restores the Constitution to its original meaning, the meaning of the founders.

If they say flag protection aligns us with dictatorships, ask them how a flag protected according to the will of a free people, a flag designed by the Father of our country, could be compared to a flag protected according to the will of a tyrant. Madison and Jefferson believed our flag should be protected, does that align them with Adolf Hitler and Joseph Stalin?

Ask them if they have ever heard of the prisoners of war of a dictatorship fashioning bits of cloth or toilet paper into a swastika or a hammer and sickle. Ask them if any prisoners of war (POWs) ever have ever said a pledge to the flag of a dictator. Tell them that Americans have done this for Old Glory in every war.

If they say flag burning does not happen often, tell them once is too often.

Ask them what frequency has to do with what is right and wrong.

To those who say the Supreme Court is the final word, tell them that in our Constitution, the people are the final word. Ask them how the Supreme Court could rule that flag burning is speech, and allow it to be burned anywhere—but on their steps.

If they quote Colin Powell that the flag amendment is not worth it to hammer a few miscreants, tell them our goal is not to hammer miscreants, our goal is to hammer the Supreme Court, they are the miscreants in this case. Remind them that General [Norman] Schwarzkopf said he considered the protection of our flag an absolute necessity, and a matter of critical importance to our nation.

Tell them that President George W. Bush said he strongly supported the flag amendment because of, among other things, a debt to your legacy of sacrifice and service.

Understanding the flag amendment

If they say they want to protect the flag but only by statute, tell them that the flag amendment will require a statute for protection, in fact it is the only way to get a statute.

Ask your representative if they are for hate crime legislation. Then ask if burning the flag is a hate crime.

If they are confused with the difference between the Legion burning a worn out flag and some one burning or defecating on a new flag, explain the word desecrate to them. It is not a flag burning amendment, it is a flag desecration amendment.

If they tell you we cannot legislate patriotism, tell them that patriotism is the last refuge of a free people and that every law we pass should inspire, should teach, should endorse, and should ensure patriotism in the people. Patriotism is simply love of country; our land, our neighbors, and our leaders. The first duty of every citizen is to be patriots and to make patriots of our children.

The notion that irresponsible, disrespectful conduct is necessary for freedom is not new but it is nonsense, not to be found anywhere in our Constitution. To separate freedom from patriotism is tragic. Patriots are the very source, often the fodder, of freedom. There is no freedom without patriots.

If they say the flag amendment reflects a tyranny of the majority, an effort to force their will on a more "virtuous" minority, ask them then if the minority of the Supreme Court, who wanted the flag protected, was more virtuous than the majority who said flag burning is speech. And ask them if the minority who would have elected their opponent, was more virtuous than the majority that elected them.

If they say we are trying to amend the Bill of Rights for the first time, ask if the Supreme Court had voted to protect the flag, would they then have amended the Bill of Rights.

If they were among those in the last election who said that every vote must count, or who during the impeachment process said we must listen to the people, remind them that is exactly what we are asking, listen to the people, let every voice count.

If they have trouble defining the American flag and feign concern about prosecuting those who burn bikinis embroidered with the flag or toilet paper marked with the flag, ask them if they would put toilet paper or a bikini on the flag of a veteran, or raise them from a flag pole during retreat.

If anyone says the flag represents the freedom to burn it, that our military died on the battlefields of the world so their flag could be burned on the street corners of America, warn them not to say that to a veteran.

An important battle

Our struggle is made more difficult because it seems not to be measurable in material terms. To find champions with the moral courage to fight for a cause without material benefit can be difficult.

It frequently seems there are precious few who will do something simply because it is the right thing to do. Many shake their heads in disbelief that we would work so hard for something that promised no monetary benefit to any one, and has in fact cost much in time and treasure for those involved.

The truth is that all the prosperity and material wealth we enjoy is the result of the sacrifices of many who gave all they had simply because it was the right thing to do. Their sacrifices certainly were not materially measurable to them but have been immeasurable to America. Our children need to know this.

To ensure that the outrageous conduct of a minority does not outweigh the will of the majority goes counter to will of the elite, but it is the right thing to do.

To begin restoring the true meaning of the First Amendment, and remind the Courts that the people own the Constitution doesn't make us a dime, but it does help stop those who would remake our Constitution. And it is the right thing to do. To return to our children a protected priceless teaching aid for patriotism won't make us rich, but it will enrich their lives. And it is the right thing to do.

To remind politicians that our laws should reflect our values has no price tag, but the results can be priceless. And it is the right thing to do.

Our bottom line is not the dollar bill, it is the Bill of Rights, it is the right of the people to define the meaning of their Constitution, and that is the right thing to do.

For those who question our efforts, our question to them is—how do you stop doing what is right?

I recall with pride a conversation between a flag skeptic and an American Legion official. The skeptic expressed alarm over how much had been spent on the Flag Amendment and asked how much more we would spend. He was told we would spend whatever it took. Why? Simply because it is the right thing to do.

Once again you are engaged in a great battle. Once again you are standing for what is right. Today you do not stand against tanks and rockets and missiles. Your wounds will not be mortal. But the wounds to America could be if your kind of patriotism dies. It is my great honor to stand with you.

14

Flag Burning Should Not Be Banned

Michael Kinsley

Michael Kinsley is a columnist for the Washington Post *and the editor of* Slate *(www.slate.com).*

A constitutional amendment banning the burning of the American flag would be a direct attack on the First Amendment. Fortunately, Congress has repeatedly failed to pass such an amendment, and support for an anti-flag-burning amendment is dwindling. Despite the claims of many congresspersons, the American flag is the least important patriotic icon, and worship of the flag is meaningless patriotism. By attempting to outlaw a form of criticism of the government, supporters of this amendment are symbolically desecrating the flag.

One of the nicest things not to have happened in recent years is a constitutional amendment against flag burning. How we have avoided this embarrassment is a mystery verging on a miracle. Raw flag idolatry was the centerpiece of George Bush the Elder's 1988 presidential campaign (the one he won).

When the Supreme Court ruled, 5 to 4, in 1989 that state laws against desecrating the American flag were unconstitutional, Congress immediately passed a federal law designed to pry away a justice or two by meeting their objections. Yet in 1990 the court threw out that law by another 5 to 4 majority. Since then, legislatures of 49 of the 50 states have passed resolutions asking Congress to rectify this dangerous situation by sending them a constitutional amendment.

A series of failed efforts

Four times, starting in 1995 and most recently [in July 2001] the House has approved such an amendment by far more than the necessary two-thirds vote. The Senate has voted twice. Both times the amendment won a majority but just barely missed two-thirds.

So, even though the citizenry—when asked—overwhelmingly wants flag-burning to be illegal, even though the spectrum of opinion on this issue among the people's elected representatives ranges (with only a few exceptions) all the way from passionate approval to fear of opposition, and even though recent law school graduates weren't even born the last time the Supreme Court was thought to be a reliable safety net for civil liberties, somehow or other and against all odds the U.S. Constitution still protects your right to burn an American flag.

[The flag-burning amendment] is a frontal attack on the spirit of the First Amendment.

And the peril to that right seems to be receding. An American Civil Liberties Union press release about the House vote crowed, without detectable irony, that this was the first time that "under 300" members of Congress supported an anti-flag-burning amendment. (The vote was 298 to 125.) The *Washington Post* gave the news one sentence in a news roundup column. The *New York Times* ran an article inside the paper with a dismissive headline labeling it a "ritual vote."

Apparently the House now counts on the Senate to save it from itself on flag burning the way the Senate depends on the House to stop campaign finance reform. In fact, the House leadership was so busy stopping campaign finance reform that the flag vote got bumped from its traditional prestige slot before the Fourth of July. First things first.

The emptiness of flag worship

How many innocent flags paid the ultimate price while members of Congress concentrated on making the world safe for soft money? That itself is a comment on all the flag-fetish one-upsmanship that accompanies this debate, in which even (or, rather, especially) opponents of a constitutional amendment must carry on about how they love and worship any piece of cloth imprinted with this design. Devotion to the flag (or something) reduced the amendment's chief co-sponsor, Representative Randy "Duke" Cunningham of California, to semi-coherence in a floor speech he posts on his Web site: "It is not hard to make this decision when one knows what their values are, and one cannot rule by 'but.' People say, well, I deplore the burning of the American flag, but. It is not hard to make the decision when one knows their values and what they are by deed heart; mind."

Well, how about this, Representative Cunningham: I don't especially deplore the burning of an American flag. (Burning of "the" flag is impossible, as there is no one flag.) Or at least I deplore it no more than I would the burning of a copy of the Declaration of Independence or the Constitution or a model of the Lincoln Memorial. The flag is the least American of our patriotic icons. Its design says nothing distinctive about us except that we were 13 colonies and are now 50 states.

Flag worship is the emptiest form of patriotism. It has no direct connection to the values that really make America exceptional. If Congress feels the need for a patriotic gesture, a better one would be to replace the national anthem. The current choice is not just empty flag worship but bellicose, impossible to sing and based on a melody not written by an American.

It is a cliche of this debate, but true nevertheless, that by attempting to forbid a form of criticism of the government, supporters of the flag-burning amendment are themselves symbolically—and it's all about symbols after all—desecrating the American flag.

A constitutional amendment by definition cannot violate the Constitution. But there's no reasonably denying that this one is a frontal attack on the spirit of the First Amendment. It's not about limiting free expression for some unrelated purpose (like preventing a protest march from blocking the streets). It's not about what might be necessary in a temporary emergency (shouting fire in that crowded theater). It's not about limits on expression in areas far removed from the Constitution's basic concern (such as regulations on commercial advertising). It's about amending the Bill of Rights for the first time ever in order to outlaw a form of criticism of the government.

I will, of course, defend to the death the right of members of Congress to call for any constitutional amendment, however fatuous and unnecessary. Especially as long as they continue to avoid actually enacting it.

15

Pornography Should Be Restricted

Jay Nordlinger

Jay Nordlinger is the managing editor of National Review.

Governments and communities can take several steps to reduce the availability of pornography. These efforts include appointing "porn czars," passing zoning laws that limit the locations of adult businesses, and using Internet filters in libraries to prevent patrons, especially children, from accessing X-rated websites. It may not be possible to completely rid society of pornography, but people with morals and common sense must not allow the nation to become further sullied.

What can be done to reduce . . . the "pervasive presence" of porn? Quite a bit, actually. We are not helpless in the face of this problem. Those who toil in the anti-pornography field say that a false sense of helplessness is one of the pornographers' best allies. People feel that they can do nothing, that all must submit, that the courts have ruled we have no choice in the matter, that this is the modern world—get used to it. Yet this is untrue. There are many things to be done, on a number of fronts: legal, policy, and social (and we will take these categories in turn, although the categories tend to blend).

The necessary traits for anti-porn campaigners

What any anti-pornography campaigner requires, first and foremost, is bravery. He must be prepared to weather a storm of abuse, including, Comstockist![1] Prude! Censor! Hater of the Bill of Rights! The anti-porn cause calls for thick skin, and both legal and moral confidence.

Consider the case of Utah and the porn czar. Yes, Utah has a "porn czar," appointed earlier [in 2001.] She is a deputy attorney general whose

---

1. Anthony Comstock was a legal reformer whose crusade led to the Comstock Law, which prohibited the mailing of indecent material.

job it is to advise communities and citizens what their rights are vis-à-vis the smut in their midst. It is, to many, a funny notion: Utah—stuffy old Mormon Utah—and a porn czar. Jay Leno duly lampooned the idea on the *Tonight Show*.

The "czar" is a seasoned prosecutor named Paula Houston, whose sexual standing was questioned early on by local reporters. It was bruited about that she—a Mormon and unmarried—was a virgin, which was too much! What would she know? But Ms. Houston replied that her sex life was irrelevant and that she would go about her responsibilities, heedless of gibes. A porn czar—someone to guide people through the thickets of the law—is an attractive idea for states, and, indeed, several of them besides Utah have been considering it. The Utah governor, Mike Leavitt, has said, "If a state legislature is looking for a way to improve the world, this is not an illogical way . . ."

Obscenity is illegal, not protected by the First Amendment.

A high moment in anti-porn resolve occurred in 1986, when the report of the "Meese Commission" came out. This was a panel charged by President Reagan with investigating pornograhy and recommending a plan of action. When Ed Meese, the attorney general, announced the commission's findings, he did so in the Great Hall of the Justice Department, in front of two Greek statues of semi-nude figures. The media had a field day with this, insisting that the setting had "stepped on" Meese's "message," leaving him a laughingstock. Here is another challenge in the war against porn: fighting the contention that, as between classical sculpture and Larry Flynt, there is hardly any difference—it's all in the eye of the beholder.

The findings of the commission were, essentially, that pornography was not necessarily a "victimless" crime and that the Justice Department needed stronger tools to prosecute it, in the form of new legislation. The commission also urged the creation of a "strike force," to go after porn's major producers and distributors. In due course, the department got both its new legislation and its strike force. And that force struck, to beneficial effect.

Politics and pornography

Pat Trueman was a key Justice Department player at the time, and he still wages the anti-porn war as director of governmental affairs for the American Family Association. As he tells it, big-time pornographers were brought to trial all over the country and, for the most part, fell like ninepins. Using both obscenity and racketeering laws, the feds were able to make a serious dent in illegal pornography. The industry quickly cleaned up its act, staying away from "child-themed" videos, and scenes featuring rape, mutilation, incest, and the like. Pornographers would take action before the law could, knowing that the authorities were alert and determined. Vigorous enforcement took place during the administration of the first George Bush as well. It was, all in all, a hazardous time for pornographers.

Then came the Clinton years—a boom time for the porn industry, a holiday from anti-obscenity prosecution. Pornographers enjoyed virtually carte blanche, as prosecutors and activists will tell you. In fact, pornographers will tell you as well. A porn producer named Mark Cromer wrote a piece for the *Nation* [in February, 2001,] in which he said, "Whatever collective pain and persecution the industry suffered during the Reagan and Bush the Elder years, when Bill Clinton rolled into the White House . . . [pornographers] saw eight years of relative green lights and blue skies." As a result, porn "has grown into a multibillion-dollar business reaching into nearly every corner of America, culturally, politically, and even economically." (This is the same explosion documented by the *New York Times's* Frank Rich).

During the 2000 presidential campaign, Adult Video News—the trade journal of porn—referred to the "benevolent neglect that the industry has enjoyed under Janet Reno" and fretted over a potential Republican victory. George W. Bush was indeed elected, and he named as his attorney general the social conservative John Ashcroft—giving pornographers a fright. "Porn Valley," out near L.A., wrote Mr. Cromer, "heard thunderclaps." And as before, pornmakers quickly went about the work of "self-censorship"—for example, there would be no "sex in a coffin." (This also from Mr. Cromer.) When asked, "What can be done?" anti-pornographers almost invariably say, before all else, simply enforce the laws already on the books. This is the answer that politicians on the stump often give when avoiding the adoption of a hard position. But it is a true and right response in this case.

Obscenity is illegal, not protected by the First Amendment. And John Ashcroft has made clear that he will—just as the porn industry feared—make anti-obscenity prosecution a priority of the Bush administration. Not even September 11 has changed that.

It matters greatly who controls the Justice Department, who controls the U.S. attorney's offices, who sets the legal and moral tone in America. As the *Nation's* journalistic pornographer put it, "George W. Bush and John Ashcroft have won half the battle simply by showing up."

Community efforts

One weapon in the anti-pornography arsenal is zoning: the practice by which cities and towns can sequester X-rated businesses, significantly improving "quality of life." This was a contributor to [former] Mayor Rudolph Giuliani's success in New York. He took on a thriving sex industry—particularly in Times Square—and walled it off. He inaugurated a "new day," as anti-porn activists said. The civil-liberties union cried censorship; the *New Republic* cluck-clucked at the mayor's "Victorian crusade." That crusade was challenged in court, and it lost a few, minor battles. Overall, though, it prevailed. Giuliani said later, "Some people romanticize the way things were [before]. . . . They think it was somehow charming to have graffiti on every wall and sex shops on every block. But remember what it was really like: Remember the fear, and the disrespect for people's rights . . . It seemed like no one cared."

Jane LaRue, senior legal director at the Family Research Council, says that communities can do more than they generally know about the porn shops that blight them, the outlets known as "sexually oriented businesses" (or SOBs). Some communities have laws on the books that are going unenforced, and some can stand to pass tougher laws. Jay Sekulow is chief counsel for the American Center for Law and Justice. His group is a rich resource for communities, even offering a "model city ordinance." There is little question that communities interested in doing so can sequester and limit porn, if not ban it outright.

One particularly important arena in the porn wars is—believe it or not—the local library: Does it have the right to block access to Internet pornography using computer filters? Should it do so? In the courts now is a federal law denying funds to libraries that refuse to block Internet porn. [As of spring 2002, that case was still in the courts.] If a practicing conservative politician has a porn issue, it tends to be this one. The American Library Association is adamantly, categorically opposed to any filtering at all.

A 1998 case in Loudoun County, Virginia, received national attention. The library there wanted to block access to Internet porn—but a district-court judge ruled that doing so would violate patrons' First Amendment rights. The principal group fighting the library called itself "Mainstream Loudoun," which is typical of the strategy employed by anti-anti-porn forces: Me mainstream, you fringe.

There is little question that communities interested in doing so can sequester and limit porn, if not ban it outright.

Libraries, however, have not proven to be completely helpless in the matter. In Minneapolis, a group of librarians filed a claim with the Equal Employment Opportunity Commission (EEOC), asserting that a library full of porn meant a "hostile work environment" for them. They were exposed to porn every day—and, worse, they were exposed to men committing lewd acts as the computer terminals. The entire atmosphere was being fouled. The EEOC found that the librarians' claims were justified, and also that they were entitled to financial redress. Librarians from around the country are registering their dismay over porn; some are even resigning. They did not sign up to work in virtual porn emporiums, and they are particularly distressed when it is difficult to separate child patrons from Internet smut.

Pornography on the Web

Some anti-porn activists have come up with an intriguing idea: Let there be a separate "domain" for Internet porn, and let all of that porn come under it. The domain would be ".xxx." So, just as we have ".edu" for educational websites, and ".gov" for governmental ones, we would have the triple X for pornography. This would be sort of an Internet zoning law, according to which all porn sites would be ghettoized. Monique Nelson, CEO of Enough Is Enough, says, "We support this for the same reason that in the physical world you can make a separate place for adult bookstores. You can regulate them. We feel that these same concepts should apply to the Internet."

Other activists disagree, however, saying that pornographers would never leave ".com" and the rest, and could never be forced to do so. Besides which, law enforcement might grow laxer with regard to Internet porn, thinking that, if it is walled off under ".xxx," it should be left alone—even if it is obscenity, or child pornography, and therefore illegal.

Illegal porn can be prosecuted, and legal porn can be discouraged.

Pat Trueman—late of the Justice Department, now with the American Family Association—notes that it is impossible to take on the entire, vast sea of pornography; better to concentrate on a few big fish. His organization, with others, has been concentrating lately on a very big fish, Yahoo, the Internet portal. Yahoo is home to thousands of sex "clubs" that disseminate manifestly illegal pornography. Mr. Trueman would like to see the company prosecuted; in the meantime, he is all for public pressure, and is directing it.

We are hardly talking here about nudies on the order of Playboy centerfolds; we are talking about . . . well, Yahoo has clubs devoted to father-daughter incest, complete with pictures, of course. There is—as the American Family Association has reported—a Forced White Wife Club, which "has photos of a man forcing a handgun into the mouth of a woman he is violating." There is an Asphyxia and More Club, featuring "photos of naked women hung by the neck, and others strangled by men." There are Real Rape Fantasies clubs. There is Rob's Necrophilia Fantasy Club, boasting "autopsy photos of naked women and medical-school cadavers. There is also a photo of what appears to be an emaciated concentration-camp victim lying naked in a mass grave next to a deceased child. A sexually suggestive caption is provided." And so on.

Mr. Trueman's group, in concert with Concerned Women for America, the Family Research Council, and others, has been harassing Yahoo without let-up. These organizations issue press releases, write letters, and generally rally public opinion. They are urging a boycott of Yahoo and its advertisers—and there is some evidence that their pressure is working. The company had planned to sell porn videos over the Net, but changed its mind in the wake of negative publicity and a letter campaign. Yet the sex clubs remain, because they are fantastically lucrative for Yahoo, and for other such portals.

Resisting the mainstreaming of porn

The "mainstreaming" of porn has meant that many big companies—some of America's most venerable—are now part of "the industry." AT&T, for example, owns the Hot Network, a cable channel that purveys hard-core porn. And then there are the major hotel chains, such as Marriott: They offer porn in all of their rooms, via cable, and this service is hugely profitable for them. Why not prosecute them, if these materials cross into obscenity? Failing that, how about old-fashioned shame? Marriott is known as a straight-laced company—what gives? Often a gust of public disapproval, or the mere prospect of a court battle, is enough to make a company desist.

Bob Rowling is a hero to the anti-porn community. Who is he, and why? He purchased Omni Hotels in 1996, and decided to remove the porn from his chain's rooms. The stuff simply offended him; he did not want to run that kind of business; and he took action, though that action cost him dearly, in revenues. Mr. Rowling is help up as an example of "corporate responsibility"—and of individual conscience, of course, too.

A brief word on advertising: It has, indeed, become "kind of porny," with the Abercrombie & Fitch catalogue—which caught Mr. Buckley's attention—serving as Exhibit A. The only way to do something about this is to object: to write in, to complain, to boycott. What is necessary here—in the words of one prosecutor/activist—is "the willingness of the average citizen to get off the couch."

In the case of Abercrombie, it appears that many customers got off their couches. The company has just announced that its next catalogue will be de-porned. Abercrombie brass explained that, in the wake of September 11, a more somber atmosphere should be maintained; but it is not unreasonable to think that public protest played some role—probably the major role—in the company's decision.

There are other anti-porn tools, other notions: Wall Street can be pressured, the mainstreaming of porn businesses resisted. The "responsible investor" can be invoked. Some groups call for more "cyber cops," officers who are trained to deal with Internet porn and its associated crimes. Before the Supreme Court now are several cases involving kids, pornography, and the Net—one of them is called *Ashcroft v. ACLU*. The anti-porn crowd stresses the need for judges who do not view the First Amendment as all-tolerating when it comes to smut.

Ultimately, our country probably needs to be "re-moralized," as the historian Gertrude Himmelfarb has written. And Americans need to care about this "pervasive presence." Think what happened to smoking in America when people generally, and elites in particular, became interested: It is now almost a pariah activity. Is pervasive porn a lesser social ill? No serious anti-porn campaigner is a utopian. None supposes that porn can be made to disappear, or that the Constitution could allow such a thing. But defeatism is unwarranted: Illegal porn can be prosecuted, and legal porn can be discouraged. In this realm, a little stigmatizing can go a long way.

One wise specialist, with close ties to the [George W. Bush] administration, says that, in the final analysis, "You have to ask, What do we as citizens want? It's the average Joe who's going to have a lot to say about this. Pornography has always been around, and always will be—but only recently has it really overwhelmed us. I mean, seven-year-olds are looking at it. We can step back. People of common sense and decent morals can say, Enough."

Yes. Enough.

16

Sexuality and Nudity Are Banned Too Frequently

Marilyn C. Mazur and Joan E. Bertin

Marilyn C. Mazur is an attorney for the National Coalition Against Censorship; Joan E. Bertin is the executive director of the NCAC.

Censors are too quick to prevent children from seeing nudity or expressions of sexuality, even when the material has artistic or educational merit. Efforts to determine what is "harmful to minors" have been part of the American tradition since the nineteenth century, but it may be time to decide whether it is constitutional or wise to deny minors access to these materials. Censors treat all nudity as obscene, despite the fact that nudity in art is often neither erotic nor offensive. Such censorship is frequently ludicrous and could lead to restrictions on scholarly writing.

> We are working up a fever making new laws against touching, and we're more scandalized by a photograph or painting showing a nipple or a penis than by the image of a starving child on a dry, dusty road.
> —Thomas Moore, *Mother Jones*, September/October 1997

> It's Sodom and Gomorrah all over again.
> —Dr. Robert L. Simonds,
> Citizens for Excellence in Education

Are Jock Sturges' photographs of nude children on the beach child pornography? Does learning about sex or reading about homosexuality cause young people to experiment with sex in ways they otherwise wouldn't? Should children be shielded from nudity in art and sex on the Internet? Can words like "masturbation" and "contraception" be banned from classroom discussions? Should parents always have the final say about what minors can read, see, and learn?

These are the issues at the center of many of the censorship wars in late 20th century America. In one sense, it's part of our tradition. From the ban on Margaret Sanger's use of the words syphilis and gonorrhea to the ban on authors James Joyce and Henry Miller, the censors have traditionally focused on sex. The debate has shifted, however. While First Amendment protection now extends to a great deal of material with sexual content—at least for adults—where children are concerned, all bets are off. As a result, most censorship wars over sex are now fought ostensibly to protect minors, and to define what is "harmful to minors."

Parents are understandably and rightly concerned about their children's sexual decisions and behavior. For some parents, sex is something reserved only for adults, limited to certain circumstances and relationships. Other adults and children have different values, goals and expectations. One rule plainly does not fit all, so how are questions about what kind of information about sex is harmful—or essential—to minors to be resolved?

Noted children's author Judy Blume has observed that "children are inexperienced, but they are not innocent." Children live in a world in which sex education is censored, but sex is glamorized in advertisements and on television, and the sexual activities of government officials are described in the morning papers and the evening news. Sexually transmitted diseases and unwanted pregnancy are other realities familiar to many teenagers. In the absence of empirical evidence demonstrating harm, perhaps it is time to reconsider whether it is constitutional—or wise—to deny young people access to information they need to make informed decisions and appropriate choices.

Defining obscenity

All but the most astute legal scholars are confused. What is the legal definition of obscenity? How is it different from pornography? What is child pornography? What is the meaning of terms like "harmful to minors," and which images are considered "indecent"?

The laws regulating material with sexual content have become increasingly complex, but sex is by no means a new subject in censorship law. Americans are heir to a tradition, fostered by religious perspectives, that viewed sex as something to be tolerated, at best—a necessary evil. In the 19th century, Anthony Comstock, founder of the New York Society for the Suppression of Vice, campaigned on the slogan "Morals, Not Art and Literature" for censorship laws to suppress erotic subject matter in art and literature and information about sexuality, reproduction and birth control. The Comstock Act of 1873 banned all material found to be "lewd," "indecent," "filthy" or "obscene," including such classics as Chaucer's *Canterbury Tales*. At one time or another, books by Ernest Hemingway, D.H. Lawrence, John Steinbeck, F. Scott Fitzgerald and a host of other literary greats have been banned under obscenity laws. Legal attitudes only began to change officially in 1957, when the Supreme Court acknowledged that sex is "a great and mysterious motive force in human life."

The legal definition of obscenity has gone through several permutations, with its current definition embodied in the 1973 case, *Miller v. California*. Material with sexual content falls outside the protection of the First Amendment if 1) the work, taken as a whole, appeals to a prurient interest in sex, as judged by contemporary community standards, 2) it portrays sexual conduct, defined by law, in a patently offensive manner, and 3) the work lacks serious literary, artistic, political or scientific value. Pornography—jokingly referred to by lawyer and author Marjorie Heins as "the dreaded 'P' word"—is not the same as obscenity. Pornography is erotic material or material that arouses sexual desire. In contrast with obscenity, pornography enjoys First Amendment protection because it does not satisfy the Miller standard, either because it has artistic, literary, historical or other social value, or because it is not patently offensive under community standards—even if some may find it so—or because the work taken as a whole does not appeal exclusively to a prurient interest in sex. Much of the material that is targeted as "indecent" is protected, at least for adults. . . .

The sexualization of nudity

Nudity—frontal or otherwise—involving sexual activity or otherwise has always offended a certain number of people. But shifting standards of what is acceptable for family viewing and of what is "harmful to minors" has lowered the threshold so that today it seems as if the body itself has become taboo. Nudity has been sexualized.

Frontal nudity is not tantamount to obscenity. Indeed, in much classic art, the nude form is neither erotic nor offensive. Nonetheless, distribution of pictures depicting nudity could be considered illegal under a variety of existing statutes and standards. Child pornography statutes have been used to target artists whose work involves children, and even parents who take pictures of their own children.

In a well-publicized case, prosecutors charged Barnes & Noble with violating state law by displaying Jock Sturges books with photographs of nude children where minors could see them. Sturges, an award-winning photographer whose work is in the Museum of Modern Art, the Metropolitan Museum of Art and the Bibliotheque National of Paris, has been targeted by Focus on the Family and Loyal Opposition, headed by Randall Terry, former leader of the anti-abortion group Operation Rescue. Some of the charges against Barnes & Noble have been dropped, after it agreed to display Sturges books higher than five and a half feet, while others are still pending. Other less visible cases have turned an innocent picture taking session into a nightmare, like that experienced by a Wayne State University art professor, who was investigated for child abuse when a janitor found a nude photograph of her three year old child in her wastebasket.

Sometimes efforts to protect minors from nudity and sexual knowledge verge on the ludicrous.

Books and photographs are not the only focus of such attacks. The Academy-Award winning film, *The Tin Drum*, was seized from the Oklahoma City library, private homes and video stores because of complaints by Oklahomans for Children and Families. The film's message, about the disintegration of central Europe during the rise of Naziism, was completely overlooked by OCAF in its attack on a few isolated and suggestive, but not explicit, scenes. A federal judge ruled that the police violated the Constitution when they seized copies of the film without a warrant or court order. The court has yet to decide whether the film violates state child pornography laws.

Another artistic casualty of the sex and censorship wars is a film version of *Lolita*, starring Jeremy Irons. True to the Nabokov novel, the film explores a man's sexual obsession with a prepubescent but precocious girl, and uses a body double in sexually explicit scenes. Although the film has been shown in Europe, *Lolita* [had] recently been unable to find a distributor in the United States, undoubtedly because of uncertainty about whether it will elicit charges of child pornography. What of *National Geographic* pictures of naked children involved in tribal rituals? Medical textbooks displaying children's genitals? Scholarly description of children's sexual fantasies? Could these be construed to violate state pornography statutes which prohibit "lascivious exhibition of genitalia"? That questions like these exist is enough to predict a chilling effect on scholarly writing and distribution of such materials. The ambiguity of the legal standards, the absence of any limiting principle that protects work with artistic, scholarly or other merit, and vagueness about what is harmful to minors all plainly contribute to censorship.

Ludicrous censorship

Most problematic is the idea that children shouldn't see a depiction of a naked body. Consider the decision by one TV station to cancel an educational film teaching women breast self-examination techniques because the broadcaster decided the material was "inappropriate for family viewing." This was the same theory on which the New York State Museum recently asked sculptor Kim Waale to remove portions of her work, *A Good Look: The Adolescent Bedroom Project*. Similarly, many libraries have "no nudes" policies for their public exhibit space, resulting in the exclusion of Robin Bellospirito's highly stylized nudes. Tulane student artist Jenny Root's nude sculpture, *Mother/Father*, was moved so it wouldn't accidentally be seen by children. The aversion to artistic representations of the human body reached new heights at Brigham Young University, where four sculptures of nudes, including *The Kiss*, were removed from a traveling Rodin exhibit. Bellospirito won her right to exhibit her paintings in court; Waale and two other artists withdrew their work from the New York State Museum in protest, but art lovers in Utah who hoped to see *The Kiss* were out of luck.

Sometimes efforts to protect minors from nudity and sexual knowledge verge on the ludicrous. On Long Island, an edition of *Where's Waldo?*, the charming mini figure puzzle book, was banned because hidden among hundreds of tiny figures crammed onto the "beach" page someone found a woman with a partially exposed breast the size of a pencil tip. In Erie, Pennsylvania, teachers used markers to block out passages of mating habits from naturalist Diane Fossey's *Gorillas in the Mist*. In New York, a teacher was disciplined for allowing other students to read a composition about a sexual experience written by a fellow student. Octorara, Pennsylvania, school officials removed a Margaret Atwood story, "Rape Fantasies," from the high school honors English curriculum.

Nudity is opposed on both sides of the ideological spectrum. Goya's famous *Nude Maja* hung on a classroom wall for 15 years until a professor charged that it was "sexually harassing." In New York City new zoning rules will exile to remote areas most sex shops, topless clubs, and bookstores featuring sexually explicit but constitutionally-protected fare. The language of the ordinance is broad enough to apply not only to "peep shows," but also to a smash hit like *Oh! Calcutta!* or an art gallery specializing in nude art; it was recently declared constitutional by a federal appeals court.

While the religious right is fueling much of the effort to ban these materials from our communities, the religious community is by no means monolithic in its views. Consider the exuberant Sister Wendy who charmed millions with her TV programs on the history of art including many nude and sexually explicit works. Consider, too, the highly touted sex education programs embraced by religious people and organizations, including American Baptists and the Unitarian Universalists. Morality is not the province of the far right, and repression of information about sex and sexuality and of images of nudity in art is not universally accepted as correct by all religions.

Organizations to Contact

The editors have compiled the following list of organizations concerned with the issues debated in this book. The descriptions are derived from materials provided by the organizations. All have publications or information available for interested readers. The list was compiled on the date of publication of the present volume; names, addresses, phone and fax numbers, and e-mail addresses may change. Be aware that many organizations take several weeks or longer to respond to inquiries, so allow as much time as possible.

American Civil Liberties Union (ACLU)
132 W. 43rd St., New York, NY 10036
(212) 944-9800 • fax: (212) 869-9065
e-mail: aclu@aclu.org • website: www.aclu.org

The ACLU is a national organization that defends Americans' civil rights guaranteed in the U.S. Constitution. It adamantly opposes regulation of all forms of speech, including pornography and hate speech. The ACLU offers numerous reports, fact sheets, and policy statements on a wide variety of issues. Publications include the briefing papers "Freedom of Expression," "Hate Speech on Campus," and "Popular Music Under Siege."

American Library Association (ALA)
50 E. Huron St., Chicago, IL 60611
(800) 545-2433 • fax: (312) 440-9374
e-mail: membership@ala.org • website: www.ala.org

The ALA is the nation's primary professional organization for librarians. Through its Office for Intellectual Freedom, the ALA supports free access to libraries and library materials. The OIF also monitors and opposes efforts to ban books. The ALA's sister organization, the Freedom to Read Foundation, provides legal defense for libraries. Publications include the *Newsletter on Intellectual Freedom*, articles, fact sheets, and policy statements, including "Protecting the Freedom to Read."

Canadian Association for Free Expression (CAFE)
P.O. Box 332, Station 'B', Etobicoke, Ontario M9W 5L3, Canada
(905) 897-7221 • fax: (905) 277-3914
e-mail: cafe@canadafirst.net • website: www.canadianfreespeech.com

CAFE, one of Canada's leading civil liberties groups, works to strengthen the freedom of speech and freedom of expression provisions in the Canadian Charter of Rights and Freedoms. It lobbies politicians and researches threats to freedom of speech. Publications include specialized reports, leaflets, and *The Free Speech Monitor*, which is published ten times per year.

Concerned Women for America (CWA)
1015 Fifteenth St. NW, Suite 1100, Washington, DC 20005
(202) 488-7000 • fax: (202) 488-0806
e-mail: mail@cwfa.org • website: www.cwfa.org

CWA is a membership organization that promotes conservative values and is concerned with creating an environment that is conducive to building strong families and raising healthy children. CWA publishes the monthly *Family Voice*, which argues against all forms of pornography.

Electronic Frontier Foundation (EFF)
454 Shotwell St., San Francisco, CA 94110-1914
(415) 436-9333 • fax: (415) 436-9993
e-mail: info@eff.org • website: www.eff.org

EFF is a non-profit, non-partisan organization that works to protect privacy and freedom of expression in the arena of computers and the Internet. Its missions include supporting litigation that protects First Amendment rights. EFF's website publishes an electronic bulletin, *Effector*, and the guidebook *Protecting Yourself Online: The Definitive Resource on Safety, Freedom & Privacy in Cyberspace*.

Family Research Council (FRC)
8801 G. St., NW, Washington, DC 20001
(202) 393-2100 • fax: (202) 393-2134
e-mail: corrdept@frc.org • website: www.frc.org

The Family Research Council is an organization that believes pornography degrades women and children and seeks to strengthen current obscenity law. It publishes the monthly newsletter *Washington Watch* and the bimonthly journal *Family Policy*, which features a full-length essay in each issue, such as "Keeping Libraries User and Family Friendly: The Challenge of Internet Pornography." FRC also publishes policy papers, including "Indecent Proposal: The NEA Since the Supreme Court Decency Decision" and "Internet Filtering and Blocking Technology."

Freedom Forum
1101 Wilson Blvd., Arlington, VA 22209
(703) 528-0800 • fax: (703) 284-3770
e-mail: news@freedomforum.org • website: www.freedomforum.org

The Freedom Forum is an international organization that works to protect freedom of the press and free speech. It monitors developments in media and First Amendment issues on its website, in its monthly magazine *Forum News*, and in the *Media Studies Journal*, published twice a year.

International Freedom of Expression Exchange (IFEX)
The IFEX Clearing House, 489 College St., Suite 403, Toronto, Ontario M6G 1A5 Canada
(416) 515-9622 • fax: (416) 515-7879
e-mail: ifex@ifex.org • website: www.ifex.org

IFEX consists of more than forty organizations that support the freedom of expression. Its work is coordinated by the Toronto-based Clearing House. Through the Action Alert Network, organizations report abuses of free expression to the Clearing House, which distributes that information throughout the world. Publications include the weekly *The Communiqué*, which reports on free expression triumphs and violations.

Morality in Media (MIM)
475 Riverside Drive, Suite 239, New York, NY 10115
(212) 870-3222 • fax: (212) 870-2765
e-mail: mim@moralityinmedia.org • website: www.moralityinmedia.org

Morality in Media is an interfaith organization that fights obscenity and opposes indecency in the mainstream media. It believes pornography harms society and maintains the National Obscenity Law Center, a clearinghouse of legal materials on obscenity law. Publications include the bimonthlys *Morality in Media* and *Obscenity Law Bulletin* and reports, including "Pornography's Effects on Adults and Children."

National Coalition Against Censorship (NCAC)
275 Seventh Ave., New York, NY 10001
(212) 807-6222 • fax: (212) 807-6245
e-mail: ncac@ncac.org • website: www.ncac.org

The coalition represents more than forty national organizations that work to prevent suppression of free speech and the press. NCAC educates the public about the dangers of censorship and how to oppose it. The coalition publishes *Censorship News* five times a year, articles, various reports, and background papers. Papers include "Censorship's Tools Du Jour: V-Chips, TV Ratings, PICS, and Internet Filters."

National Coalition for the Protection of Children & Families
800 Compton Rd., Suite 9224, Cincinnati, OH 45231-9964
(513) 521-6227 • fax: (513) 521-6337
website: www.nationalcoalition.org

The coalition is an organization of business, religious, and civic leaders who work to eliminate pornography. It encourages citizens to support the enforcement of obscenity laws and to close down neighborhood pornography outlets. Publications include the books *Final Report of the Attorney General's Commission on Pornography, The Mind Polluters*, and *Pornography: A Human Tragedy*.

People for the American Way (PFAW)
2000 M St., NW, Suite 400, Washington, DC 20036
(202) 467-4999 or 1-800-326-PFAW • fax: (202) 293-2672
e-mail: pfaw@pfaw.org • website: www.pfaw.org

PFAW works to promote citizen participation in democracy and safeguard the principles of the U.S. Constitution, including the right to free speech. It publishes a variety of fact sheets, articles, and position statements on its website and distributes the e-mail newsletter *Freedom to Learn Online*.

Bibliography

Books

Richard L. Abel — *Speaking Respect, Respecting Speech*. Chicago: University of Chicago Press, 1998.

Randall P. Bezanson — *Speech Stories: How Free Can Speech Be?* New York: New York University Press, 1998.

Fred H. Cate — *The Internet and the First Amendment: Schools and Sexually Explicit Expression*. Bloomington, IN: Phi Delta Kappa Educational Foundation, 1998.

Ann Curry — *The Limits of Tolerance: Censorship and Intellectual Freedom in Public Libraries*. Lanham, MD: Scarecrow Press, 1997.

Richard Delgado and Jean Stefancic — *Must We Defend Nazis?: Hate Speech, Pornography, and the New First Amendment*. New York: New York University Press, 1997.

June Edwards — *Opposing Censorship in the Public Schools: Religion, Morality, and Literature*. Mahwah, NJ: L. Erlbaum Associates, 1998.

Mike Godwin — *Cyber Rights: Defending Free Speech in the Digital Age*. New York: Times Books, 1998.

Alan Haworth — *Free Speech*. London: Routledge, 1998.

Thomas R. Hensley — *The Boundaries of Freedom of Expression and Order in American Democracy*. Ohio: Kent State University Press, 2001.

Nat Hentoff — *Living the Bill of Rights: How to Be an Authentic American*. New York: HarperCollins, 1998.

Alan Charles Kors and Harvey A. Silverglate — *The Shadow University: The Betrayal of Liberty on America's Campuses*. New York: Free Press, 1998.

David Lowenthal — *No Liberty for License: The Forgotten Logic of the First Amendment*. Dallas: Spence, 1997.

Charles Lyons — *The New Censors: Movies and the Culture Wars*. Philadelphia: Temple University Press, 1997.

Robert M. O'Neil — *Free Speech in the College Community*. Bloomington: Indiana University Press, 1997.

Bruce W. Sanford — *Don't Shoot the Messenger: How Our Growing Hatred of the Media Threatens Free Speech for All of Us*. New York: Free Press, 1999.

Timothy C. Schiell — *Campus Hate Speech on Trial*. Lawrence: University Press of Kansas, 1998.

James Weinstein   *Hate Speech, Pornography, and the Radical Attack on Free Speech Doctrine*. Boulder, CO: Westview Press, 1999.

Nicholas Wolfson   *Hate Speech, Sex Speech, Free Speech*. Westport, CT: Praeger, 1997.

Periodicals

Doug Bandow   "Free to Be Stupid," *Ideas on Liberty*, March 2002.

Ethan Bronner   "Big Brother Is Listening," *New York Times Education Life*, April 4, 1999.

Jim D'Entremont   "Preachers of Doom," *Index on Censorship*, July/August 1999.

Dissent   "Minors and the First Amendment," Fall 1999.

Marjorie Heins   "Screening Out Sex," *American Prospect*, July/August 1998.

Mark Y. Herring   "X-Rated Libraries," *Weekly Standard*, July 5–July 12, 1999.

Nancy Herzig and   "Pornography, Censorship, Sexuality," *Against the*
Rafael Bernabe   *Current*, March/April 1997.

Lester H. Hunt   "Repealing the Codes of Silence," *Liberty*, May 1999.

Issues and   "Pornography," September 25, 1998.
Controversies on File

Molly Ivins   "Even Racists Have Right to Free Speech," *Liberal Opinion Week*, September 29, 1997.

Kenneth Jost   "Libraries and the Internet," *CQ Researcher*, June 1, 2001.

Roger Kimball   "A Little Censorship Would Be Good for Hollywood," *Wall Street Journal*, October 2, 2000.

Gara Lamarche   "The Price of Hate," *Index on Censorship*, March/April 1999.

David Lowenthal   "The Case for Censorship," *Weekly Standard*, August 23, 1999.

Nation   "Speech and Power," July 21, 1997.

Ralph R. Reiland   "Muzzling the Speech Cops," *Regulation*, Fall 1999.

Laurence H. Tribe   "The Internet vs. the First Amendment," *New York Times*, April 28, 1999.

Keith Wade   "The Internet: Parental Guidance Preferred," *Ideas on Liberty*, February 2000.

Julia Wilkins   "Protecting Our Children from Internet Smut: Moral Duty or Moral Panic?" *Humanist*, September/October 1997.

Wilson Quarterly   "One Cheer for Censorship," Winter 2000.

Index

93